Vegetarian Pastability

Lizzie Spender is an actress, playwright and cookery author. She is the daughter of the late Sir Stephen Spender and lives in north London with her husband, Barry Humphries.

Vegetarian Pastability

Lizzie Spender

Illustrations by Michele Tranquillini

ff

faber and faber
LONDON · BOSTON

For Oscar and Rupert Humphries

First published in 1997
by Faber and Faber Limited
3 Queen Square London WC1N 3AU

Typeset by Faber and Faber Ltd
Printed in England by Clays Ltd, St Ives plc

© Lizzie Spender, 1997
Illustrations © Michele Tranquillini, 1997

Lizzie Spender is hereby identified as author of this
work in accordance with Section 77 of the Copyright,
Designs and Patents Act 1988

A CIP record for this book
is available from the British Library

ISBN 0–571–17874–X

10 9 8 7 6 5 4 3 2 1

Contents

More Vegetarian Dishes

Oriental Vegetable Dishes

Oriental Fish Dishes

Acknowledgements

I would like to thank all those kind and enthusiastic friends and acquaintances who provided me with encouragement and recipe ideas for this book, many of whom I have written about in individual recipes; but also including Sandy Forsyth for her Oriental ideas; 'George' Etsuji Takabayashi, my favourite Japanese chef; Minoru and Kieko Yoshihara from our favourite Japanese restaurant in London, Wakaba in the Finchley Road.

As always, Francesca and Idelma and Idelma's daughter, Betty Valentine, who in addition helped me with typing and organisation of the book. My other Italian mother figure, Giovanna Toppi from my favourite Italian restaurant in the world, Machiavelli in Sydney, Australia. My friend and brilliant cook, Jean Moore.

David Meredith, who has lugged so many carrier bags laden with ingredients for pasta recipes back from our favourite Waitrose. Mrs Roche, manageress of the self-same Waitrose in the Finchley Road.

Louise Arthur, our assistant, who performed miracles with the computer to get the book ready on time.

My good friend, Rosamond Freeman-Attwood, who by now is adept at eating pasta, writing down the recipe *and* writing down dialogue for our stage plays – all at once.

Last, but by no means least, my husband Barry Humphries and my step-sons Oscar and Rupert Humphries for their constant enthusiasm and, above all, seemingly inexhaustible appetites for my culinary inventions. And not forgetting Dame Edna, who claims that her Megastar performances owe much to the energising powers of my pasta.

Foreword

My formative toddler years were spent crawling about the floor of a kitchen in St John's Wood, London, presided over by Francesca, our Italian cook, and Idelma, my Italian nanny. Both had been 'kidnapped' by my parents from Lake Garda in northern Italy, where we had lived for a few months when I was just a baby whilst my father finished working on a volume of poems. Idelma and Francesca were not that taken by London, and were especially unimpressed by the new-fangled washing machine that my mother had bought; they said they would have much preferred Lake Garda at the back door – to scrub the sheets on the stones.

I can think of no better place for a small child to grow up than in the warmth of a kitchen with the reassuring chatter of Italian voices, frequent cuddles and the aromas of Italian food. No wonder I worship the Italian cuisine! I have a strong need to share this childhood nurturing and to feed my friends whenever they come to the house. What better way than with a big bowl of steaming pasta, served on a hand-painted Majorcine peasant plate? However unexpected the visit, there is always something in the fridge or store cupboard that will make a fabulous sauce.

What I love about pasta is its simplicity and versatility. Just by throwing some spaghetti into a pot of boiling water and rustling up a few additional ingredients you have a delicious meal for your friends, your family, or even just yourself. Follow the basic Italian rules, choose good-quality Italian pasta, cook it in *a lot* of fast-boiling, salted water (a common mistake is to use far too little water), drain it when it is still 'al dente', and you cannot fail – even if all you put on the pasta is some good-quality olive oil, crushed garlic and some herbs or grated cheese.

Ten years ago, when I wrote my first book, pasta was just beginning its journey towards being one of the most popular modern 'convenience' foods. In those days there was still a widely held prejudice that pasta meant Spaghetti Bolognese, usually consisting of overcooked, mushy spaghetti with a tasteless meat and tomato sauce, or Macaroni Cheese, likewise with overcooked macaroni and a tasteless cheese sauce. There was also a feeling that pasta was a second-best product, a cheap option and that if you invited people to the house and fed them pasta they would feel cheated or slighted.

Since the mid-eighties, things have changed dramatically. Now, with the fantastic ranges of pastas and ready-made sauces available in the shops and the imaginative combinations available in restaurants, cafés and cookery books (not to mention on television cookery programmes), the world is waking up to what the Italians have always known – that pasta is the ideal food: tasty, healthy, practical, economical and with limitless possibilities in its combinations with other foods.

Introduction

The Pasta Diet – Stamina, Weight Loss and Health

In my view pasta is the best food you can find to help you lose weight. And the reasons are simple. Pasta is the great stamina-boosting food. It is eaten by athletes, including marathon runners, before a race. This is because it is a complex carbohydrate – so even a small quantity provides the body with a steady and sustained flow of energy over an extended period of time. This 'energy' gives you 'willpower' because it keeps at bay the sudden hungers and energy lows which cause one to eat too much.

When the blood sugar level in one's body falls, one naturally craves food to restore it, and unfortunately, in many cases, sugar. Sugar is the worst thing possible to eat; it is high in calories and has no nutritional value whatsoever. It creates a false sugar 'high', at which point the body stops making its own sugar, so when the effect of the consumed sugar has worn off the body is left with a 'low' and a craving for more sustenance.

Fat is also the enemy of the dieter. We all know about the evils of animal fats; not only are they high in calories but also they clog up the arteries. Unfortunately, even olive and other vegetable and nut oils, although considerably better for you than animal fats, are equally high in calories. Butter, olive oil, nut, seed, vegetable oils and even margarine are all 100 calories a tablespoon (15 ml spoon), which is why you will find that I use them extremely sparingly in my recipes! I know that a lot of modern diets claim that calories are not the point but, personally, I don't believe them.

Pasta on its own is not high in calories – only about 100 calories an ounce (25 g) when weighed uncooked, and 33 calories an ounce when cooked.

And so an ideal health and/or weight loss diet would contain a little pasta (even a couple of ounces), once or twice a day for energy and to maintain willpower; a low-fat sauce on the pasta

1

for 'taste'; a large quantity of steamed or raw vegetables for fibre, vitamins, amino acids; plenty of fruit. (Most vegetables, especially the green ones, are extremely low in calories; fruits are higher.) And then, for non-strict vegetarians, I would include some fish and cheese for protein. Vegetarians, and especially vegans, have to balance their diets carefully to provide themselves with the necessary proteins. Good-quality dried pasta made from durum wheat also contains a fairly high percentage of protein – 13 per cent to 16 per cent compared to the 10 per cent in bread flour. Unfortunately, some of the lower quality fresh pastas are made from a flour with a low protein content. It is the high protein percentage which gives good-quality pasta that springy quality which makes it easier to handle.

Types and shapes of pasta

The following is a list of the pastas I have used in this book, with their Italian names and English equivalents where appropriate, and is included as a guide should you come across the Italian for a pasta which I have named in English.

Italian	English
cannelloni	
conchiglie	shells
farfalle	bows, butterflies
fettucine	ribbon noodles
fusilli	twists
lasagne	
linguini	(a flat spaghetti)
maccheroni	macaroni, pasta tubes
penne	quills
penne rigate	ribbed quills
rigatoni	large ribbed pasta tubes
spaghetti	
spaghettini	(thin spaghetti)
tagliatelle	ribbon noodles
capellini	
vermicelli	angel hair (or very thin spaghetti)

How to Cook Pasta

How much to cook

I have tried to give in each recipe guides to appropriate quantities, but you must also take into account the appetites of guests and how many other dishes and courses you are serving. A very rough thumbnail guide would be 50 grammes (2–2½ ounces) per person as a starter, or 100–125 grammes (4 ounces) per person as a main course. Bear in mind that the larger, heavier pasta shapes will appear to be a smaller serving when cooked that the same weight of smaller, lighter, thinner pasta. For example, 100 g of a thick-walled rigatoni will seem, when cooked, a great deal *less* than 100 g of vermicelli (angel hair) or even a delicate, small quill. Bear in mind too that large, healthy appetites might require *larger* quantities of pasta.

How much water?

It is essential to cook the pasta in *plenty* of boiling water, otherwise it becomes sticky, soft and glutinous on the outside while still not properly cooked on the inside. You will need enough water for the pasta to move very freely, even when it has expanded towards the end of cooking, and if you can see the starch in the water (it will become slightly cloudy) then quickly boil a kettle and add more. I recommend using the following table as a guideline.

| Pasta | | Water | |
ounces	grammes	pints	litres
Up to 4	Up to 125	1½–2	1
4	125	2	1–1½
8	225	4	2½
16	450	8	4½
24	675	12	7
32	900	16	9

I possess one medium-size pan (4 pints) in which I cook 1–2 main course servings, and a couple of huge pans (16 pints) in which I cook larger quantities, using whatever quantity of water is necessary.

To cook the pasta

It really hardly matters what sauce you put on your pasta – open your fridge door and be inventive – but what is absolutely essential is that you use the right sort of good-quality Italian pasta and cook it the classic Italian way, using plenty of water, and taking it off the heat and draining at the 'al dente' stage.

Bring the water to a fast boil then add to the water approximately 1 x 5 ml spoon (1 teaspoon) of salt per 100–125 g (4 oz) pasta and ½–1 x 5 ml spoon (½–1 teaspoon) oil – cheap vegetable oil. Then wait for the water to return to a fast rolling boil before adding the pasta, otherwise you will increase the tendency for the pieces to stick together. Throw in the pasta *all at once*, and immediately stir well with a wooden spoon to separate the pieces. It is at this point that the pasta is in danger of congealing, so make sure the pieces are moving freely.

Cook until 'al dente', that is, firm (not hard) to the bite. It takes practice to know when pasta is ready. Even now, I still nearly always ask for a second opinion. It is almost impossible to predict how long a particular pasta will take to cook, which is why I have not given cooking times in the recipes. Thick, solid pieces, such as large pasta tubes or shells, will obviously take much longer than a fine spaghetti, but it is very dangerous to try to invent any rules of thumb as there are too many variables. Don't rely on the packet to give you the correct cooking time. Getting it right is really a matter of standing over the pan and, when the pasta is nearly ready, tasting every 45 seconds until it is. Pasta can overcook in just a matter of seconds, especially one that is not made from 100 per cent durum wheat semolina. I do *not* believe the old adage, 'Throw a piece of spaghetti at the wall and if it sticks the pasta is ready.' In my experience, it all depends on how sticky your kitchen walls are!

When the pasta is 'al dente', drain it immediately into a

colander standing in the sink. Then pick up the colander with its contents and shake it well to remove excess water before returning the pasta to the saucepan or a preheated serving dish.

I like to put the sauce and the pasta back in a pan over a low flame. I do this to ensure that the sauce is well integrated with the pasta and that the dish is served piping hot. Italians consider this to be rather sacrilegious; they prefer to mix the pasta with the sauce in the serving dish. But then Italian families are trained young to be at the table waiting with fork poised for the arrival of the pasta dish. In my own experience, as soon as dinner is ready, everyone disappears to make urgent phone calls and so on.

For the Oriental noodles, follow the instructions in the recipes, remembering that the Chinese egg noodles need cook for only a couple of minutes, and the cellophane noodles for literally seconds.

Timing your cooking
For most dishes the pasta and the sauce should be cooked simultaneously, so that the pasta is ready with the sauce. You will soon learn how to synchronise them, but don't despair if you don't. For most dishes it is possible to keep the sauce waiting as long as it is reheated gently while you are draining the pasta – and is served hot. If you use good-quality Italian pasta and follow my working instructions religiously, then it is also possible to keep the pasta waiting whilst you finish off the sauce. Just drain and return to the pan with a 15 ml spoon (1 tablespoon) of olive oil or a small knob of butter. Mix in the sauce as soon as possible, heat through over a low flame, and then serve immediately.

Occasionally, especially when entertaining friends, you may prefer to make the sauce well in advance. Reheat gently, and bear in mind you may need to add a little more liquid at the last minute.

Precooking lasagne and cannelloni
Cooking lasagne and cannelloni tubes is tricky. It's very easy to end up with burnt fingers and the pasta on the floor, or with a

mass of congealed lasagne leaves impossible to separate. Many people swear by the 'oven-ready' type, although a few are brave enough to use the traditional kind without precooking. When I have tried this it has always been slightly too glutinous for my taste, and has taken a *long* time to cook in the oven.

To precook lasagne and cannelloni (my method)
First fill a large saucepan with 8–10 cm (3–4 inches) of water. Bring the water to a fast boil and add ½ x 5 ml spoon (½ teaspoon) salt and ½ x 5 ml spoon (½ teaspoon) oil. Bring back to a fast boil, and then slip in the lasagne leaves (or cannelloni tubes) three at a time, stirring well with a wooden spoon to separate them. After 2–3 minutes, when the pasta is still very 'al dente' (i.e. slightly undercooked), remove the pieces one by one using a slotted spoon and the wooden spoon – and taking care not to let the pasta slip out of your grip! Dip each leaf or tube into a shallow bowl containing cold water and a couple of 15 ml spoons (tablespoons) of oil. Then put to one side onto a clean tea towel on top of a draining board, spread out and overlapped like a deck of cards, until ready to use. Idelma, my Italian nanny, always pats the lasagne leaves dry with a clean dishcloth, to ensure that one is not bringing extra water to the recipe.

I have found the best way to make lasagne or cannelloni dishes is to prepare the sauce before cooking the pasta. I can then lay the precooked pasta in the baking dish as soon as it is removed from the boiling water and allow it to stand for a minute or so, adding the sauce as I go. This method avoids having pasta leaves spread all over the kitchen.

Fresh Pasta

As I said in *Pastability, A Second Helping*, I hardly ever use fresh pasta. I would be the first to say 'fresh is best', but unfortunately this is not always the case for pasta. Most of the products available in England are in my view inferior to the better brands of dried pasta, such as F. lli de Cecco and Barilla (see page 12).

What never ceases to amaze me is the blind faith with which 'fresh' pasta is proudly served in this country on the assumption that, as it is 'fresh' and more expensive, it just *has* to be better. Often enough on the plate in front of me – even in very smart restaurants – I find either a barely disguised quantity of indigestible, undercooked flour and water dough, or an overcooked, soggy mass. Yes, I'm exaggerating, but either way it sits in the stomach like a lead balloon! Of course, if you find a local shop that supplies a wonderful fresh pasta, easy to cook and serve and simply delicious, then who am I to argue with that? And in spite of my attitude, I do believe that the pastas served on the chilled counters of supermarkets have improved over the past few years. My advice is to try them out and then decide what kind of pastas you prefer.

There was an aristocratic lady living in Milan in the 1930s who was famous for the marvellous fresh pasta served at her table. Nobody could discover the secret, least of all the lady herself until, one day, walking unannounced into her kitchen, the truth was revealed. Her chef was rolling out the pasta against his bare and sweating chest!

As I said before, the best pasta is made from durum (hard) wheat flour, which contains 13–16 per cent protein, as opposed to the 10 per cent to be found in bread flour. The big pasta companies buy up the best wheat before it is even harvested. I'm told de Cecco buy their wheat from California, which might explain why their pasta seems to grow to about twice its original size while cooking! Some of the fresh pasta sold in Britain is made from the low-protein bread farina. It is the protein content in the flour which gives the pasta the characteristic springy, slightly chewy quality it has when cooked to the 'al dente' stage. The problem with fresh or dried pasta made without this high-protein flour is that it appears to pass from raw and undercooked to soft and slightly mushy with no intervening 'al dente' stage, and so not only is less appetising to eat, but also cannot be reheated and eaten later, or eaten cold. If you *do* decide to make your own pasta, it is well worth going to the trouble of finding durum wheat flour. I was astounded to find that my local super-market (Waitrose on the Finchley Road in London) stocks it on the Italian produce shelves near the pasta sauces.

Storing and cooking fresh pasta

Genuine fresh pasta keeps in the fridge for two or three days. It is possible to freeze it – in which case it keeps for up to six months – and to cook it directly from the freezer. For taglia-telle or spaghetti I would recommend the following method of freezing. Spread the pasta out flat on a plate (or plates) to a thickness of not more than 3 cm (about an inch). Put the plate and pasta into a plastic bag and freeze. When the pasta is frozen, remove the plate, seal the pasta into the plastic bag, and return it to the deep freeze. If you freeze the pasta as a solid mass in a bag, when the time comes to cook it there is a danger the outside strands will reach the 'al dente' stage while the centre of the lump is still completely frozen.

Fresh pasta takes considerably less time to cook than dried. It is dangerous to try to predict how long, as all pasta is different. Count on a third to half of the time the equivalent dried pasta would take – usually less than 3 minutes, and a maximum of 5. Watch it like a hawk as it can overcook in a matter of seconds.

Which Type of Pasta?

The types of pasta I have suggested are those which are most readily available in the shops, and for each recipe I have suggested a type or types I know from experience will go well with that particular sauce. Of course, you do not have to use the pasta I have specified – you can substitute one type for another according to your own preference and what is to hand.

With Italian cooking there are traditional combinations of pasta type and sauce which are probably more consistently adhered to in restaurants than in private houses. There are also theories which I have heard discussed more frequently in

America than in Italy: that the simple oil sauce clings best to the pasta strand, such as spaghetti and linguini; that the more complex, heavier sauces stick to the ridges of the ribbed, tubular rigatoni; that the quills have a nice, succulent way of retaining the more liquid sauces. The twists, I suppose, do a bit of everything. Remember that a heavy pasta is the best complement to a heavy sauce.

How to Serve Pasta

It is essential with most pasta dishes that they be served *very* hot, and as soon as they are ready. It is therefore advisable to round up those about to eat the pasta and persuade them to sit at the table just *before* the dish is actually ready! Plates should be well warmed in advance, and it is important, if you are intending to transfer the pasta from the pan to a serving dish, to preheat the dish too.

I do abhor the habit of dolloping grated cheese onto every kind of pasta *before* tasting and deciding whether or not this particular dish would be improved by the taste of Parmesan, or Cheddar, or whichever cheese you are offering. Please try to persuade your guests to taste first!

Oriental Pasta

Chinese egg noodles
Thin, brittle, yellow noodles, dried in 13-cm (5-inch) looped skeins. Sold in packets in Chinese and Oriental provision shops, and some supermarkets. You can substitute a fine Italian egg pasta, a 'vermicelli' or 'angel hair'. F. lli de Cecco do an excellent box of little 'birds' nests' of vermicelli, but use the Chinese noodles if you can. Incidentally, Sainsbury's too has recently begun to stock these noodles fresh.

Cellophane noodles or 'vermicelli' (Thai name: Wun Sen)
Fine noodles made from the starch of green mung beans. Sometimes known as 'glass' noodles. As the name suggests, they are transparent. They are soaked in cold water for 20 minutes, and then dunked in boiling water for just 30 seconds.

9

Available as above. Do not be put off by their rather slippery texture and taste. You will quickly grow to love them.

Rice noodles, rice sticks or rice vermicelli
(Thai names: Sen Yai, Sen Lek, Sen Mee)
As the names suggest, noodles in different sizes but all made from rice. Again these noodles are soaked for 20–30 minutes and then dropped for less than a minute into boiling water.

Soba noodles
These are the Japanese 'buckwheat' noodles, available in Japanese supermarkets. You can always substitute buckwheat noodles from your health food shop.

Leftovers

Make the most of leftovers – cold vegetables, ends of cheeses. All can be utilised in the concoction of delicious, original pasta sauces.

Leftover cold pasta can always be used the next day. Some dishes taste excellent cold. Others can be heated up as follows. Add a little liquid – cream, white wine, oil, butter, or combinations of these – and warm gently in a pan, stirring with a wooden spoon and adding more liquid if necessary. Another possibility is to mix in some béchamel sauce, sprinkle grated cheese on top and bake in the oven.

Improvisation

Allow yourself to be led by your taste buds, and make a pasta sauce out of anything that strikes your fancy! My recipe ingredients are, in a sense, only suggestions. There is practically no ingredient (apart from the pasta itself and a little butter, oil or liquid) which cannot be omitted or substituted for another. I make pasta sauces with whatever I find in the fridge or larder, or whatever looks fresh and is a good buy in the shops. I consider it a creative challenge to be presented with somebody else's fridge or cupboard – however bare – and asked to concoct a pasta dish.

Standby Ingredients

If you keep a selection of dried pastas and some basic sauce ingredients you will be able to throw together a pasta meal at short notice and without a quick dash to the shops. The following list includes all the basic standbys, with items I regard as absolutely essential marked with an asterisk.

The store cupboard

tinned Italian plum tomatoes (Waitrose, Safeway's and Sainsbury's brands are all good)

tomato purée (available in tubes, jars, tins or cartons to be kept in the fridge once opened. Transfer remaining contents of a tin to another receptacle)

tins of fish: anchovies; salmon; sardines; *tuna fish; clams; crab; mussels (but not those preserved in a vinegary liquid)

olives and capers

dried red chillies; chilli powder

dried herbs (especially marjoram, oregano, sage, thyme, basil)

sea salt

garlic

whole black peppercorns

onions (do experiment with the unusual varieties if you come across them – the little shallots for example, or the large, dark-red onion)

longlife cream

pesto sauce (the jar should be kept in the fridge after it has been opened)

sun-dried tomatoes (and/or sun-dried tomato paste)

pine kernels

wine

good olive oil (it is essential to use a top-quality olive oil. Most of the big supermarket chains stock a good selection at reasonable prices. I would strongly recommend Waitrose Extra Virgin oil, a bargain at less than £7 a litre)

vegetable or nut oil (the Oriental dishes require an oil without flavour – something simple like sunflower or safflower. Never use olive oil in Oriental dishes. However, a few drops of sesame oil can impart a very appropriate and delicious taste. Be guided by your taste buds)

pasta (a selection of packets of your favourite brand of pasta in different shapes and types. I prefer the make F. lli de Cecco di Filippo, recognisable by its bright turquoise and yellow packets. It is available in Italian delicatessens, and I make a point of stocking up whenever I find it. I also use and highly recommend Barilla, which is more easily available. Whatever the brand, always use a pasta which is made from 100 per cent durum wheat semolina. It will not only be more nutritious than a pasta made with a softer flour, or a mixture of flours, but will also be easier to cook. It will remain at the 'al dente' stage for a little longer, thus lessening the hazard of your perfectly cooked pasta turning into a congealed and soggy mess somewhere between draining and serving)

vegetable stock cubes or powder (I use a Swiss product made by Marigold called 'Swiss vegetable bouillon powder' which comes in a green tin and is available at good health food stores)

The fridge
eggs

single and double cream

crème fraîche and/or fromage frais

butter

fresh vegetables

fresh, ungrated Parmesan cheese and/or fresh Cheddar or Gruyère cheese

Italian Mozzarella, Italian ricotta (now available in most big chain supermarkets, such as Waitrose and Sainsbury's) *(chilled) pesto sauce* (available in Waitrose, Sainsbury's, etc.)

The freezer
If you have a freezer, I would recommend storing a selection
of the following items:

leaf spinach

peas

broad beans

Parmesan cheese
This is best bought in a lump and kept wrapped in paper or
foil in the fridge. Buying Parmesan can be a painful experience, for it is expensive. Console yourself with the fact that a
little goes a long way. Be generous, although I know it hurts
when a decent-sized lump is put on the scales in the shop and
the price comes to more than £5. Having gone to all the trouble to serve excellent pasta with an exquisite sauce it really is
worth going the whole hog and getting the grated cheese
right. It is *not* worth bothering with the little packets and
round boxes of ready-grated Parmesan: the stuff is tasteless
and expensive – and does *not* go a long way.

Grate the Parmesan as and when you need it. I prefer to
leave a lump of Parmesan with a grater on a plate on the
table. This is not only economical, but it discourages people
from the deplorable habit of throwing a spoonful of Parmesan onto the pasta before they have tasted the dish and
decided whether or not that particular dish needs it. Parmesan has a strong flavour and can drown the delicate taste of
some dishes. This practice also allows your diners to decide
whether they prefer their cheese grated fine or coarse.

Oriental Ingredients

Nowadays, the basics of Oriental cooking are widely available in most parts of the world. However, there are
ingredients which are essential in the preparation of Thai
food which seem to be obtainable only in Thai provision

shops. Once you have the ingredients at hand, Thai dishes are on the whole very simple and quick to prepare, and a trip to a Thai shop is always fun providing you go armed with a list of the essential ingredients you require. Here is a list of the basic Oriental necessities. Check first with the recipes you are intending to make to find out your exact requirements. The asterisks denote Thai ingredients available, in my experience, only in Thai shops – the rest you can find in supermarkets or local Oriental provision stores, of which there seems to be a constantly growing number in all parts of the world.

aubergine (some Oriental shops stock a very nice round aubergine, about an inch or two in diameter and green in colour. If you can't get hold of any, then substitute the usual purple/black variety)

**basil, holy* (not quite like the basil the Italians use. The leaves are darker and smaller, and the taste not quite so sweet)

bean curd (tofu) (very nutritious and non-fattening, with a bland taste which grows on you. Nowadays available all over the place. The firmer the better. Keeps for a couple of days in the fridge)

cardamom pods (little grey/green husky pods. Inside are the most delicious black seeds. Available from supermarkets)

chillies (red or green. Can be bought fresh. I usually use the dried red variety, which are mega-strong! Be careful never to wipe your eyes after handling one. You can substitute chilli powder or chilli oil)

coconut milk (bears as little resemblance to the stuff inside the coconut you win at a funfair as skimmed milk does to condensed milk. It took me years to get to grips with this one! I used to try melting down bars of solid coconut cream, and manufacturing coconut milk out of desiccated coconut and milk, and the conclusion I have come to is that there is no substitute for a decent tin of the stuff. I buy Chaokrung coconut milk from the Thai shop. Remember that, as with full-cream milk, the cream and the milk separate so you must decant the whole can into a bowl and beat with a fork. Once opened it keeps in the fridge, but not for long. Any coconut milk left over can be frozen for next time)

coriander, fresh leaves (available nowadays in more and more shops. Even the big supermarkets stock it. Absolutely delicious and a must for Oriental cooking. Try it in salads)

*curry paste, red and green (one of the great joys of the Thai food stores, apart from the charming Thais who work in them, is that they stock the basic curry pastes ready made up. In my local shop it is possible to buy them in handy-sized plastic sachets. For the recipes in this book I have used two: green curry paste and red curry paste. Keeps in the fridge, but make sure you put it in a sturdy, airtight container)

fish sauce, fish gravy (you don't need a lot of this. In fact, I think most Thai restaurants in this country use a bit too much for our Western palates, unaccustomed as we are to fermented fish gravy, either in theory or in practice. The first time I ever cooked with it I panicked and threw the contents of the pan down the sink, fearing that it would irrevocably taint my precious saucepan. But I have found that by buying a fairly innocuous variety, the colour and consistency of a good brandy, and using it in moderation, it is a valuable addition to Oriental cooking)

galangal (or kha) (very useful for the Thai coconut curries. Looks a little like ginger root. Tastes a bit soapy on its own)

garlic

ginger (fresh root, nowadays available almost everywhere and an essential ingredient in Oriental cooking of all kinds)

*kaffir lime leaves (also known as citrus leaves) (in my view, the very powerful flavour of these leaves is the key to Thai cuisine. Buy them in packets only at the Thai shop, and keep them in the fridge, well wrapped up, or else the strong flavour will taint other items of food. If you are keeping them more than a day or two, freeze them. Cut them with kitchen scissors)

lemon grass (available in very small packets from some

forward-thinking supermarkets, and of course – most economically – at the Thai shop, in the form of stalks or a kind of giant grass. The flavour is very characteristic of Thai cooking)

mirin (cooking sake [rice wine])

nori and yakinori (Japanese seaweed available in packets of sheets from a Japanese provision store)

oil (Oriental dishes require an oil without flavour – something simple like sunflower or safflower. Never use olive oil in Oriental dishes. However, a few drops of sesame oil can impart an appropriate and delicious taste)

palm sugar (available in Oriental shops. I sometimes substitute a thick, tasteless honey, or brown sugar)

peanuts (avoid the salted cocktail variety. Thai shops do a bag of raw peanuts, which I then roast in a pan in the oven. To crush, put them in a plastic bag and beat with a rolling pin)

sake (rice wine)

sesame seeds (available from most supermarkets)

shrimp, dried (I usually pick up a small packet when I'm in the Thai shop)

soy sauce (of course, an essential part of Oriental cuisine. Beware of the cheap imitations containing strange substances and monosodium glutamate. I buy Kikkoman, which is a Japanese product. Light soy sauce is lighter in colour and flavour though still quite salty. Kikkoman make this also)

soy bean sauce (less potent than soy and sweeter. Buy from Thai or Oriental shops)

spring onion (seems to appear in Oriental recipes almost as frequently as garlic)

spring roll pastry (available in frozen sheets in Thai shops or some Chinese and Oriental shops. Keep in the deep-freeze)

wood ear mushrooms (wood fungus – Hed Hunu) (used in Thai and Japanese dishes, available in the dried form from Oriental provision stores)

Equipment

The essential basic equipment necessary for cooking pasta dishes is minimal. A large saucepan in which to cook the pasta itself (*very* large if you are intending to entertain more than four or five people), and a large colander for draining it; a medium-sized frying pan and medium-sized saucepan for preparing sauces; a couple of wooden spoons for stirring (and possibly serving) the pasta and sauce; a large bowl or plate, which can be preheated, for serving the pasta at table; a couple of ovenproof dishes or pans for cooking lasagne and other baked pasta dishes; and a cheese grater, a garlic squeezer and a sharp knife for chopping vegetables.

For the Oriental dishes there is no doubt that a wok is extremely useful. If you don't have one, put it on your Christmas/birthday list instantly! With the wok will probably come a large wooden spatula for stir-frying, although you can also use a wooden spoon. A sharp knife and kitchen scissors are very helpful for all the fine chopping, and personally I like to eat all Oriental food with chopsticks.

Béchamel Sauce

Béchamel sauce is used in a number of the recipes. Rather than repeat the instructions for making it each time it occurs, I have given the basic recipe at the end of the book (page 224) and included the quantities needed for individual recipes in the ingredients lists.

Salt and Pepper

I have not specified salt and pepper except in recipes where I believe the addition of sea salt and freshly ground black pepper is essential for the final taste. This is because, for reasons of health and/or personal taste, so many people nowadays don't use salt and/or pepper.

Personally, I *would* use sea salt and freshly ground black pepper in virtually *all* the recipes in this book except those in the Oriental and Kids sections.

Vegetarian Dishes

Quick and Easy

- Take trouble to make sure that you are cooking with enough water. If water goes cloudy, boil up a kettle and add more boiling water.
- If you think the pasta and sauce might turn out a little dry, some people suggest draining the pasta quickly and leaving in some of the cooking water.
- Instead of serving freshly grated Parmesan, try putting a lump of Parmesan and a grater on the table so people can grate their own.
- *Always* taste the pasta before adding grated cheese. It often doesn't need it, especially any pasta with fish, and that includes anchovies.
- Always feel free to *substitute*. That's what all the best Italian cooks do – they make the sauce with whatever is in the house, the garden or available that week in the market.
- Almost all my ingredients are optional, apart from the pasta itself! Experiment with what you have and what you like, and invent your own sauces, using my recipes as a base.
- The secret of a good tomato sauce is never burning the garlic. It should always retain its white colour. If the garlic goes crispy and brown, take it out and start again!
- Adjust the chilli according to taste. It is very hard to give an accurate measurement as chillies vary. The saying is, the smaller the hotter.
- Always remember to use lots and lots of fast-boiling, lightly salted water to cook your pasta.
- If your pasta is soggy and tasteless, or continues cooking after you have drained it, here are some possible reasons:

    You've overcooked it;

    You've used an unreliable brand. Use good-quality Italian pasta, for example, de Cecco or Barilla (not Buitoni) or experiment with your local supermarket produce until you find one that works well for you.
- If your pasta is soft on the outside but still hard in the centre it could be that you are not using enough water to cook it in.
- Find a brand of pasta that you like and stock up on it. I recommend F. Ili de Cecco, Barilla (not Buitoni) and Marks and Spencer dried fresh egg pasta.
- If you use a good brand of pasta and cook it correctly (with lots of salted, boiling water until it is 'al dente') it will not go mushy on you – you can even drain it, toss it with a spoonful of oil and heat it up later or the following day.
- Feel free to experiment. Be brave. Open the fridge and make a sauce with whatever falls out.
- Stock up on store cupboard standbys from the Introduction and you will always be able to dish up a meal for friends at short notice.
- If you are partial to one of the spicy tomato sauces make extra and freeze in cupfuls. Add a little extra oil after defrosting.
- Buy herbs in pots at your local supermarket and keep them on your kitchen windowsill.
- Buy pesto sauce from the chilled section of the supermarket and freeze in ice cube trays. Decant into a plastic bag and keep frozen for future use.
- I heard Delia Smith the other day on television saying, 'Life is too short to roast a red pepper.' All I can say is I disagree – totally – and I am quite a lazy cook and believe in dishes that can be prepared quickly with the minimum amount of fuss. I *don't* find roasting red peppers a hardship. It's easy-peasy and quick. Just follow my instructions.

1 Spaghettini with lightly fried courgettes and herbs

I adore thyme. Along with basil and tarragon, it is one of my favourite herbs. I buy it fresh from the supermarket in a little pot, leave it on the kitchen windowsill, and even add a few leaves to green salads. One of its advantages is that being so pungent, a little goes a long way.

This is a wonderfully pure and simple dish. The slightly burnt flavour of some of the better cooked slices of courgette give it its 'kick'.

As an optional extra, try adding 50 g (a couple of ounces) cubed Mozzarella (or another mild cheese) and toss for a few moments with the pasta just before serving.

For 2 main course or 4 starter size helpings, use:

4 x 15 ml spoons (4 tablespoons) olive oil
450 g (1 lb) courgettes, finely sliced
½ fresh chilli, finely chopped (to taste)
one pinch sea salt (to taste)
2 cloves garlic, crushed
225 g (8 oz) spaghettini
1 or 2 x 5 ml spoons (1 or 2 teaspoons) fresh thyme or
    oregano, finely chopped, *or* substitute 1 x 5 ml spoon (1
    teaspoon) dried thyme or oregano
freshly milled black pepper

Fry the sliced courgettes with the chilli and sea salt over a medium to high heat in 3 x 15 ml spoons (3 tablespoons) of the oil, until about three-quarters have turned golden (and a few dark brown), adding the garlic about halfway through. (If you try to get all the courgettes golden you'll probably end up having to fish out lots of little charred bits, so I always stop whilst the going is good.)

Meanwhile, cook the pasta in plenty of salted, boiling water until 'al dente', drain, and return to the pan. Pour on the remaining 1 x 15 ml spoon (1 tablespoon) of olive oil, and then toss over a medium flame with the fried courgettes, pepper and herbs (and cubed cheese, if using), until heated through. Serve immediately on its own (it doesn't really need Parmesan).

2 Wholewheat twists with Boursin cheese

A delicious dish that is extremely quick and easy to prepare. Experiment with other types of herbed cream cheeses.

For 3 main course helpings, use:

    200 g (1 x 7½ oz) Boursin cheese with chives and garlic
    15 g (½ oz) butter
    4 x 15 ml spoons (4 tablespoons) single cream
    salt and pepper
    325–350 g (12 oz) wholewheat twists

Crumble the Boursin into a bowl and put aside. Melt the butter in a pan, stir in the cream and seasoning, and keep warm on a very low heat.

Meanwhile, cook the pasta in plenty of salted, boiling water. Drain when 'al dente' and return to the pan on a very low heat. Pour on the warm, melted butter and cream, stir in the Boursin cheese, and continue cooking until the cheese melts and coats the pasta.

Serve immediately.

3 Quills with Stilton, sage and cream

This is an excellent recipe for using up tired, leftover bits of Stilton, especially if you have indulged in a whole or half Stilton over Christmas. (You could mix in some other leftover cheese to make up the quantity if necessary.) It is also possible to substitute another strong, blue-veined cheese for the Stilton, such as Gorgonzola, Dolcelatte or Roquefort.

I like to serve this dish with a green vegetable or mixed salad, as its colour is a little bland. For the same reason you could consider using one of the coloured or wholewheat pastas.

For 4 main course helpings, use:

25 g (1 oz) butter
8 leaves fresh sage, *or* ½ x 5 ml spoon (½ teaspoon)
   dried sage
175 g (6 oz) Stilton, grated or crumbled
150 ml (¼ pint) single cream
salt and pepper
450 g (1 lb) quills
grated fresh Parmesan (optional)

Melt the butter. Add the sage and cook over a very low heat for a minute. Stir in the cheese, cream and seasoning, and continue cooking until the cheese has melted.

Meanwhile, cook the pasta in plenty of salted, boiling water until 'al dente'. Drain and put back into the pan. Add the Parmesan cheese to the sauce at the last minute before pouring it over the pasta. Stir the sauce in well. Serve very hot with additional grated Parmesan on the side.

4 Quills with vodka, tomato and cream

I find pasta tubes of one sort or another particularly suitable for this recipe as they have a way of retaining the sauce most successfully, making this a very succulent dish. I would recommend quills for all the vodka sauces, but you could use any other short-tube pasta.

I have a rule of thumb for the quantity of vodka in these recipes, reminiscent of a certain tea advertisement in the sixties and seventies – one spoon of vodka per person and one for the pot!

For 8 starter size helpings, use:

    50 g (2 oz) butter
    6 x 15 ml spoons (6 tablespoons) tomato purée
    425 ml (¾ pint) single cream
    9 x 15 ml spoons (9 tablespoons) vodka
    salt and pepper
    450 g (1 lb) quills

Melt the butter over a low heat. Stir in the tomato purée and the cream. Remove from the heat and add the vodka and seasoning.

Meanwhile, cook the pasta in plenty of salted, boiling water until 'al dente'. Drain, and put back into the pan or into a preheated serving dish. Reheat the sauce if necessary, taking care not to let it boil, and mix into the pasta.

Serve immediately.

Note: If you want to burn off the alcohol content, add the vodka to the butter, mix in the tomato purée, and allow to bubble for a few minutes.

5 Saskia's twists with anchovies, sun-dried tomatoes, red pepper, chopped herbs and roasted pine kernels

My brother, Matthew Spender, is a painter and sculptor and lives in the depths of Tuscany with his wife, Maro Gorki, the painter. Their two gorgeous daughters, Saskia and Cosima, now live in London. My niece Saskia works as a producer on independent films. She is a brilliant cook and kindly invented this recipe for me.

Eating pasta in Tuscany is so simple. They just put an enormous pot onto the stove, throw in the spaghettis (they always seem to refer to them in the plural) and then wander into the garden and return with handfuls of fresh herbs or whatever else is growing. They pour on a quantity of their own olive oil, some crushed garlic and toss it together with the coarsely chopped herbs – serving it at the huge wooden kitchen table (above which prosciutto hams hang from beams) with a huge hunk of Parmesan and a grater and black pepper grinder.

For 4–5 starter size or 3 main course size helpings, use:

    2 x 15 ml spoons (2 tablespoons) olive oil
    100 g (4 oz) pine kernels
    8 anchovies
    3 cloves chopped or crushed garlic
    1–2 chillies, coarsely chopped
    ½ red pepper, sliced
    100 g (4 oz) sun-dried tomatoes, coarsely chopped
    2 x 15 ml spoons (2 tablespoons) oil from the sun-dried
        tomato jar
    350 g (14 oz) twists
    chopped, fresh marjoram, parsley, coriander, or mint
        (if not available, substitute dried oregano)
    grated Parmesan on the side (optional)

Dry-fry the pine kernels in a non-stick pan, turning constantly until they are lightly roasted.

Put the anchovies into a saucer and cover with milk. Leave for a minute, drain away the milk and coarsely chop.

Sauté the pine kernels, anchovies, chopped garlic, chillies and red pepper in the oil for a minute. Add the sun-dried tomatoes and the 2 spoons of oil from the sun-dried tomato jar and sauté for another minute.

Meanwhile, cook the pasta in plenty of salted, boiling water until 'al dente', then drain the pasta and toss it in the pan with the sauce and the chopped herbs. Serve piping hot with (optional) coarsely grated Parmesan on the side (but please taste before adding cheese).

6 Spaghetti with oil, garlic and herbs

This dish, made with the maximum amount of garlic (raw, of course!) and parsley, is the Italian version of the quick sandwich or toasted cheese snack . . .

Raw garlic is very good for you and is especially beneficial if you feel a cold coming on. If you are worried about the effects of raw garlic on your breath, the theory is that the parsley cancels this out, but please don't hold me accountable!

For 2 main course helpings:

3 x 15 ml spoons (3 tablespoons) olive oil,
   or 50 g (2 oz) butter
1–3 cloves garlic (according to taste and the size of the cloves), crushed*
225 g (8 oz) spaghetti
1–2 x 15 ml spoons (1–2 tablespoons) fresh chopped herbs (parsley, basil or coriander) or ½ x 15 ml spoon (½ tablespoon) dried herbs
salt and freshly ground black pepper (preferably sea salt)

Sauté the garlic in the oil *very gently* on a low heat for a minute or so. If allowed to get too hot, the garlic will burn and become bitter, turning deep gold or brown. If this happens, strain off the garlic pieces and begin again, using the same oil but fresh garlic. (Italian purists don't even attempt to cook the garlic – they just put raw garlic straight onto the pasta with the oil.)

Meanwhile, cook the pasta in plenty of salted, boiling water until 'al dente'. Drain and put back into the pan. The herbs should be added to the oil (or butter) just before it is mixed into the pasta. Pour the oil, garlic and herbs over the pasta, season with salt and pepper, and continue cooking for a minute or so, stirring well.

*If you find this amount of garlic more than you can take, leave the cloves whole and remove them from the oil just before pouring it over the pasta.

7 Spaghetti with oil, garlic and chilli

In Italy this is traditionally the dish that men prepare for their friends after a long night on the tiles. Whether this is because they do not dare wake their wives at such a late hour and in a drunken state, or whether it is because the dish has therapeutic properties against a hangover, I don't know. Whatever the reason, it is an excellent store cupboard standby for a quick supper, good for late on a Sunday night to eat in front of the television.

For 2 main course helpings, use:

> 3 x 15 ml spoons (3 tablespoons) olive oil
> 1–3 cloves garlic (according to taste), crushed
> 1–2 dried red chillies, chopped, *or* ½–1 x 5 ml spoon (½–1 teaspoon) chilli powder*
> salt and pepper
> 225 g (8 oz) spaghetti (or quills or bows)
> grated Parmesan or Cheddar cheese (optional)

Sauté the garlic and the chilli in the oil over a *very gentle* heat (see comments on 'Spaghetti with oil, garlic and herbs', page 28). Add salt and pepper to taste.

Meanwhile, cook the pasta in plenty of salted, boiling water until 'al dente'. Drain and put back into the pan. Pour the oil, garlic and chilli over the pasta and stir in well.

Serve very hot with grated cheese on the side if you like.

*The amount of chilli used in this recipe is entirely according to taste: if you like very hot food then, obviously, use a lot of chilli. But don't forget, when tasting the sauce, that the blandness of the pasta will dilute the power of the chilli quite considerably.

8 Bows with broccoli, Brie and walnuts

Very tasty and very easy. A good way of using up the Brie (or Camembert) before it passes its sell-by date. You could also substitute a nice soft blue cheese such as Dolcelatte.

I actually made this dish the first time using fiorelli, a dried 'fresh' egg pasta made by Marks and Spencer which I would heartily recommend. It's quite delicious and behaves exactly as good pasta should behave.

I also used broccoli combined with courgettes – the *yellow* courgettes available in some large supermarkets – cut into little rounds and then halved. The yellow with the green of the broccoli and white of the pasta looked particularly attractive. I used a little chilli and a dash of Worcestershire sauce on my husband's servings for a little extra 'zing' and sprinkled over a few chopped chives which were growing in a pot on my windowsill (courtesy of Tesco this time, though many supermarkets stock them).

If you're feeling extravagant throw on a few asparagus tips, cutting off the woody portion of the stalk and steaming until soft but not mushy.

For 2 light main course helpings, use:

325–350 g (12 oz) broccoli florets (or substitute courgettes or cauliflower, or a combination)
1 x 15 ml spoon (1 tablespoon) olive oil
2 x 15 ml spoons (2 tablespoons) butter
3 large spring onions (optional), finely sliced
1 clove garlic, crushed
225–275 g (8–10 oz) bows (or frills)
75 g (3 oz) Brie, skinned and cubed
40 g (1½ oz) walnuts, broken

Steam or parboil the vegetables until cooked (still on the crisp and colourful side, and definitely *not* mushy; broccoli takes longer than courgettes).

Sauté the spring onion (if using) and garlic in the butter and oil for just a few seconds in a frying pan large enough to hold the pasta as well.

Meanwhile, cook the pasta in plenty of salted, boiling water until 'al dente'. Drain quickly, and toss in the frying pan with the oil, garlic, spring onion, parboiled vegetables, Brie and walnuts. Serve with freshly grated Parmesan on the side.

9 Wholewheat twists or shells with stir-fried vegetables

Ideally you should stir-fry the vegetables in a wok. If you don't possess one, use a large, heavy frying pan or saucepan. The process of stir-frying is, in a nutshell, to sauté and turn the vegetables continuously with a wooden spoon over a high heat so that they cook quickly without burning and retain a slightly crispy texture. Slice the vegetables *before* you begin to cook, and leave them ready on separate plates. The stir-frying process is so fast that you won't have time to prepare them as you go along.

Feel free to substitute other vegetables in season in whatever quantities and proportions you choose. Courgettes, turnips, cauliflower, Chinese cabbage and spinach would all be appropriate. You could even make the whole dish using just one vegetable. I always use a Japanese soy sauce made by a company called Kikkoman. Beware inferior substances as they have all sorts of strange additions including monosodium glutamate; and, at the worst, the texture (and taste) of tar.

For 4 main course helpings, use:

    2 x 15 ml spoons (2 tablespoons) nut, vegetable oil
        or sesame seed oil
    1 clove garlic, crushed
    pinch salt
    1 x 5 ml spoon (1 teaspoon) fresh ginger root, finely
        chopped or grated (optional)
    ½–1 small dried chilli, to taste (optional)
    225 g (8 oz) carrots, finely sliced
    225 g (8 oz) leeks, finely sliced
    100–125 g (4 oz) broccoli, finely sliced
    100–125 g (4 oz) mushrooms, finely sliced
    2 x 15 ml spoons (2 tablespoons) vegetable stock or water
    1 x 15 ml spoon (1 tablespoon) soy sauce

1 x 5 ml spoon (1 teaspoon) sugar
450 g (1 lb) wholewheat twists or shells

Sauté the garlic, salt, ginger and chilli in the oil for just a minute over a fairly high heat. Turn up the heat and throw in first whichever vegetable you think will take the longest to cook. Stir-fry for a minute or so, then add the next vegetable. Continue this way until all the prepared vegetables have been added to the pan. Stir-fry all the vegetables together for another couple of minutes before adding the stock, soy sauce and sugar. Continue frying and stirring for a little longer until the vegetables are cooked but still crispy, adding more water or stock if necessary.

Meanwhile, cook the pasta in plenty of salted, boiling water until 'al dente'. Drain, and either put into the wok with the vegetables, or back into the pasta pot with the stir-fried vegetables on top. Heat through and mix together thoroughly.

Serve with grated cheese on the side. I'm not convinced cheese goes with soy sauce, but some people like the combination.

10 Spaghetti with tarragon and lemon

It goes without saying that you must decide you like the taste of
tarragon before trying this dish! A good, light lunch dish especially
enjoyable after a too late and too rich supper the night before.
There are two versions really: either with just the grated lemon
rind or with the addition of lemon juice and Parmesan (the lemon
juice is a little strong on its own, but the Parmesan cancels that
out). I would recommend using spaghetti or spaghettini.

For 2 light helpings, use:

   175 g (6 oz) spaghetti or spaghettini
   1½ x 15 ml spoons (1½ tablespoons) good olive oil
   grated rind 1 lemon
   2 x 15 ml spoons (2 tablespoons) fresh tarragon, coarsely
      chopped or torn up with your fingers
   1 x 15 ml spoon (1 tablespoon) freshly squeezed lemon
      juice (optional)
   1 x 15 ml spoon (1 tablespoon) freshly grated Italian
      Parmesan, or more, to taste (optional)

Cook the pasta in plenty of salted boiling water until 'al
dente'. Drain, and put back into the pan with the oil, grated
lemon rind, and tarragon. Toss, then add the lemon juice if
using and toss again. Serve on preheated plates with the
Parmesan cheese, if using, on the side, or sprinkled on top.

11 Bows with mashed courgettes, Parmesan and basil

This recipe was given to me by Mariluis Pallavicino, an Italian friend. She insists that this dish should be made with neither chilli nor garlic but, addict that I am, I cannot resist adding a smidgen of both. If basil is not available then simply make the dish without it, and you can substitute marrow or even broccoli for the courgettes.

A light and refreshing dish, but if you crave something spicier then mash in a couple of anchovy fillets.

For 2 light main course helpings, use:

> 275 g (10 oz) courgettes, sliced
> 1 x 15 ml spoon (1 tablespoon) olive oil
> 5–10 leaves of fresh basil, torn into small pieces
> 1 clove garlic, crushed (optional)
> 1 very small dried red chilli, crumbled (optional)
> 25 g (1 oz) Parmesan cheese, medium grated
> 175 g (6 oz) bows (or similar shapes)
> freshly ground black pepper

Boil the courgettes in lightly salted water for at least 5 minutes, until soft. Put on a plate and mash with a fork. Stir in the oil and basil leaves, then the garlic, chilli and anchovy, if using; add two-thirds of the grated cheese.

Meanwhile, cook the pasta in plenty of well-salted, boiling water until 'al dente', drain, and put back in the pan with the courgette mixture. Toss over a low flame for a couple of minutes until well mixed and heated through. Serve with the remaining cheese sprinkled on top, and with plenty of freshly ground black pepper.

12 Gian Carlo Menotti's 'spaghetti dei poveri' with tomatoes, parsley and garlic

This pasta sauce was invented in Naples during the Second World War at a time when meat was scarce. Supposedly, the flavour of the burnt garlic and the texture of the parsley give the impression of a 'ragù' or meat sauce. I don't agree! But it certainly is tasty.

The recipe was given to me by the great Italian composer Gian Carlo Menotti. He prepared it for us on a cold stormy night at his magnificent house in Scotland.

For 2 main course helpings, use:

6 x 15 ml spoons (6 tablespoons) olive oil
3 cloves garlic, sliced*
400 g (14 oz) tinned chopped tomatoes
50 g (2 oz) parsley, finely chopped
225 g (8 oz) spaghetti, or spaghettini
1 fresh Italian Mozzarella (100–150 g/4–5 oz),
   chopped into small cubes (optional)

Sauté the sliced garlic in the hot oil (in a small pan with a lid) until well browned. Strain out the garlic, and put the oil back in the pan. Transfer the tinned tomatoes into a shallow bowl (a cereal bowl will do). Reheat the oil on a medium flame until very hot. Very quickly remove the lid, slide in the tomatoes and slam the lid back on immediately, taking care not to be burnt by the spitting hot oil. The tomatoes will cool down the oil considerably, so it will be safe now to add the parsley. Simmer on a fairly high flame for about 10 minutes, stirring occasionally, and taking care not to let the sauce stick.

Meanwhile, cook the pasta in plenty of well-salted, boiling

*Garlic addicts might like to consider recycling the garlic. In other words, slicing it before cooking, putting aside after straining the oil, then serving it sprinkled on top of the finished dish. You could also add a freshly squeezed clove to the sauce at the same time as adding the parsley.

water until 'al dente', drain and then put back in the pan with the tomato sauce. Add the chopped Mozzarella, if using, and then toss over a low flame for a couple of minutes until well mixed and heated through, when the Mozzarella should be nice and gooey. Serve immediately.

13 Gnocchetti* with spring greens, red pepper and Mozzarella

This recipe was given to me by an Italian friend (and brilliant cook), Emmalisa Marcozzi Rozzi. Emmalisa lives in London and cooks pasta regularly for her husband and their friends. She uses F. lli de Cecco pasta, or else buys it fresh from Harrods, and invents sauces out of locally available ingredients. Both the red pepper and the Mozzarella are my optional additions to the original recipe.

For 3–4 light main course helpings, use:

450 g (1 lb) spring greens
3 x 15 ml spoons (3 tablespoons) olive oil
1 medium sweet red pepper, chopped
1–2 cloves garlic, crushed
1–2 small dried red chillies, crumbled or finely chopped
225 g (8 oz) gnocchetti, or other small pasta shapes
1 fresh Italian Mozzarella (100–150 g/4–5 oz),
    chopped into small cubes

Slice the greens across into strips about 1 cm (½ inch) wide, then slice the other way across into small squares. Boil in lightly salted water for 8–10 minutes (depending on how tough the leaves are). Drain well, then put aside.

Sauté the chopped red pepper with the garlic and chillies in 2 x 15 ml spoons (2 tablespoons) of the oil until the pepper has softened. Add the cooked greens and sauté together for a couple of minutes.

Meanwhile, cook the pasta in plenty of well-salted, boiling water until 'al dente'. Drain, and toss together with the remaining spoon of oil. Add the pasta and Mozzarella to the vegetable mixture, and heat thoroughly on a medium flame until the dish is piping hot and the cheese pleasantly gooey. Serve immediately.

*Gnocchetti Sardi: a small pasta shape (2 cm/¾ inch long) made by F. lli de Cecco, resembling a hollow caterpillar.

14 Rigatoni with red pepper, tomatoes, blue cheese, sun-dried tomato paste and tarragon

As with most of my recipes I suggest substituting ingredients if you find you do not have the noted ingredients available. I love the taste of tarragon, but if you don't have any then choose another tasty herb, or even a dried herb. My favourite dried herb is oregano. Remember to use less if using a dried herb, or a very strong herb such as finely chopped thyme or rosemary.

For 3 main course helpings, use:

- 2 x 15 ml spoons (2 tablespoons) olive oil
- 1 clove garlic, crushed
- 1 small dried chilli, to taste (optional), crumbled or chopped
- 125 g (4 oz) onion, finely chopped
- 1 red pepper (finely sliced, or roasted and then sliced, if preferred)
- 12 cherry tomatoes, cut in half (or substitute, chopped, any fresh tomato)
- 325 g (12 oz) rigatoni
- 3 x 15 ml spoons (3 tablespoons) puréed sun-dried tomatoes (or substitute 1 x 15 ml spoon (1 tablespoon) tomato purée, 1 x 15 ml spoon (1 tablespoon) sun-dried tomatoes, chopped, 1 x 15 ml spoon (1 tablespoon) oil from sun-dried tomato jar)
- 125 g (4 oz) blue cheese or goat's cheese, cubed
- 2 x 15 ml spoons (2 tablespoons) coarsely chopped fresh tarragon (to taste), *or* substitute any available fresh herbs
grated fresh Parmesan

Sauté the garlic, chilli and onion in half the oil until softened. Add the red pepper and tomatoes and continue to cook for another minute or so.

Meanwhile, cook the pasta in plenty of salted, boiling water until 'al dente'. Then drain the pasta and return it to the pan and toss over a low flame with the remaining tablespoon of oil and the sun-dried tomato purée (or substitute mixture). Add the rest of the cooked ingredients and the blue cheese.

Toss together and serve piping hot with the chopped tarragon sprinkled on top and grated fresh Parmesan on the side.

15 Quills with green beans, courgette, mushrooms, tomatoes, butter beans, pesto sauce and fromage frais

Most supermarkets sell excellent bottled pesto sauces nowadays. Some (for example, Waitrose) even sell fresh pesto in plastic containers in the chilled section. Feel free to experiment with different vegetables, or even left over cold vegetables from the fridge, when trying this recipe.

For 3 main course (or 4 small) helpings, use:

    100 g (4 oz) green beans
    1 large courgette
    3 x 15 ml spoons (3 tablespoons) olive oil
    1 clove garlic, chopped
    1 dried chilli, chopped
    100 g (4 oz) mushrooms, sliced
    100 g (4 oz) tomatoes, coarsely chopped
    220 g (8 oz) tinned butter beans, or substitute cannellini
        beans, drained
    325 g (12 oz) quills, or bows
    salt and pepper
    2 x 15 ml spoons (2 tablespoons) bottled pesto sauce
    4 x 15 ml spoons (4 tablespoons) fromage frais
        (or crème fraîche)

Put plenty of salted water on for the pasta and bring to the boil. Drop in the green beans and the courgette and leave simmering for 5 minutes. Remove with a slotted spoon and leave to cool a little. Slice or chop the courgette and chop the beans in 2 cm (1 inch) lengths.

Sauté all the vegetables (including the parboiled courgette and green beans), the chopped garlic and the chilli, in 2 x 15 ml spoons (2 tablespoons) of the oil, on a medium heat, until the vegetables start to turn golden.

Meanwhile, cook the pasta in the boiling water until 'al dente'. Then drain the pasta and return it to the pan with the remaining spoon of oil and the 2 x 15 ml spoons (2 tablespoons) pesto sauce. Toss until the pasta is coated with the pale green sauce. Add the vegetables and salt and pepper to taste, then toss again.

Serve piping hot with a spoonful of the fromage frais on the top of each serving. Sprinkle on a few fresh basil leaves. Hand around a wedge of Parmesan cheese and a coarse grater for people to help themselves.

16 Tagliatelle with carrots, broccoli, walnuts, blue cheese and cream

Very simple taste, quite rich. I tend to use the egg pastas (for example, tagliatelle) when I am making a sauce with butter and cream. You could substitute all cream or crème fraîche rather than using both, and leave out blue cheese if you like and substitute Gruyère or Emmenthal or more Parmesan.

For 2 main course or 4 starter size helpings, use:

2 large carrots (225 g/8 oz)
225 g (8 oz) broccoli
20 g (¾ oz) butter
100 g (4 oz) onion, cut into quarters and then finely sliced
4 x 15 ml spoons (4 tablespoons) crème fraîche
2 x 15 ml spoons (2 tablespoons) single cream
sea salt and freshly ground black pepper
225 g (8 oz) tagliatelle
50 g (2 oz) soft blue cheese (Gorgonzola or Cambozola), chopped in small cubes
100 g (4 oz) walnuts, coarsely chopped
grated Parmesan

Put plenty of salted water on for the pasta whilst you peel the carrots and wash the broccoli. As soon as the water boils, drop in the carrots and the broccoli and simmer for two or three minutes just to soften. Remove from the water with a slotted spoon. (The water will remain slightly coloured, but don't worry, it won't really affect the pasta colour.) Slice the carrots *finely*, and cut the broccoli into separate florets. Put aside.

Sauté the onion in the butter in a lidded pan over a low heat, until the onion has softened. Add the sliced carrots and broccoli florets, put on the lid and cook over a low heat for a few minutes, turning frequently. Add the crème fraîche and cream, sea salt and freshly ground black pepper, and a little of the pasta water (a couple of tablespoons) if the sauce seems too dry for your liking.

Meanwhile, cook the pasta in the boiling water until 'al dente'. Then drain the pasta and return it to the pan. Add the sauce, the cheese and the nuts, and toss together over a low flame. Serve immediately, with the grated Parmesan on the side.

17 Bows with bok choy, optional cherry tomatoes and garlic

This recipe was invented by my husband, Barry Humphries, as a 'cold cure' because, as you can see, it incorporates a huge quantity of garlic! We're both totally addicted to garlic, for its exquisite flavour and also for its medicinal qualities. It is reputed to be good for cleansing the blood and warding off all sorts of illnesses, including the common cold.

Bok choy is a kind of Chinese cabbage, available in many of the bigger supermarkets, such as Sainsbury's or Waitrose. If you can't find bok choy you could easily make this recipe substituting spinach, savoy cabbage or even extra tomatoes for the bok choy.

For 2 main course helpings, use:

2 bunches bok choy
3 x 15 ml spoons (3 tablespoons) olive oil
8 cloves garlic, peeled and coarsely chopped
1 small dried chilli, coarsely chopped
12–14 cherry tomatoes, sliced in half (optional)
225 g (8 oz) bows
about eight basil leaves (optional)
freshly grated Parmesan

Put plenty of salted water on for the pasta and, when it is boiling, drop the bunches of bok choy into the water for a couple of minutes to soften. Fish them out and then chop them into 1 cm (½ inch) slices.

Put the oil in the pan on a medium to high heat. Throw in the garlic and chilli, and sauté for just 30 or so seconds, watching the garlic very carefully. If you overcook the garlic, it will turn brown and bitter and you may as well remove it with a slotted spoon and start again. Add the bok choy and tomatoes and sauté for another few minutes, until the tomatoes soften.

Meanwhile, cook the pasta in the salted, boiling water until 'al dente'. Then drain the pasta and return it to the pan. Add the sauce and toss together over a low flame. Tear the basil into small pieces and sprinkle over the pasta just before serving. Serve immediately, with the grated cheese on the side.

18 Quills with butter, anchovies, garlic, red pepper, walnuts and crème fraîche

This dish is exquisite and incredibly easy. It works particularly well as a starter and is special enough to serve at a dinner party. You could substitute tagliatelle, or even home-made tagliatelle, for the quills. If you don't like, don't have, or are sick of the sight of red peppers, try substituting finely chopped spring onions (raw or sautéed in the butter, adding them just before the anchovies) or a couple of 15 ml spoons (tablespoons) of almost any fresh green herb, finely chopped. I would recommend dill, chives, basil, tarragon or a combination of these.

You can serve this dish with freshly grated Parmesan on the side but bear in mind that the Italians believe you should never serve cheese with a pasta dish which incorporates fish. I would recommend putting a lump of really good-quality Parmesan on the table with the grater but suggesting that your fellow diners taste the pasta before attacking the cheese grater.

For 4 starter size helpings, use:

1 large or 2 small red peppers
25–50 g (1½ oz) butter
8 anchovy fillets, soaked in a bit of milk
2 cloves garlic, crushed
75–100 g (3 oz) walnuts or pecan nuts, coarsely chopped
   or broken
6 x 15 ml spoons (6 tablespoons) crème fraîche
225 g (8 oz) small quills
12 leaves basil (or substitute tarragon or parsley),
   torn into pieces

Place the whole peppers on the grill pan (removing the rack if necessary), with the peppers almost touching the heating element, and grill on a high heat on all four sides until the peppers turn completely black. Allow to cool and then peel off the black, burnt skin. Cut into halves, remove the stalk and seeds and then slice the slightly cooked and softened pepper into strips and lay out on a plate. Put aside.

Melt the butter in a small pan over a low flame, taking care it doesn't burn. Add the anchovies and crushed garlic and stir until integrated with the butter. Add the walnuts (or pecan nuts) and crème fraîche and stir together.

Meanwhile, cook the pasta in plenty of salted, boiling water until 'al dente'. Then drain the pasta and return it to the pan.

Toss pasta with sauce and roasted red peppers – or if you want the dish to look a little more showy, then toss the pasta with the sauce, place on a dish and lay the red pepper strips evenly over the pasta. Sprinkle on the basil and serve immediately.

19 Quills with courgettes (or green beans), blue cheese, herbs and cream

An Italian friend of mine, Agnese Bourchi, who used to work as a housekeeper for the composers Gian Carlo Menotti and Samuel Barber, makes a wonderful risotto combining courgettes and blue cheese, so I have stolen her idea of this combination to invent a pasta dish.

It's worth paying real attention to the cooking of the courgettes or green beans. You certainly don't want them too crisp and raw, but you also don't want them impossibly mushy or faded.

For 2–3 main course helpings, use:

> 450 g (1 lb) courgettes, cut lengthwise in eighths, and then cut into 5 cm (2 inch) lengths *or* substitute 325 g (12 oz) green beans cut into 7.5 cm (3 inch) lengths
>
> 2 x 15 ml spoons (2 tablespoons) olive oil or butter
>
> 100 g (4 oz) onion, very finely sliced or chopped
>
> 1 clove garlic, crushed
>
> 1 chilli (to taste) chopped or crumbled (optional)
>
> 1 x 15 ml spoon (1 tablespoon) fresh sage, chopped, *or* substitute tarragon, basil or chives
>
> 100 g (4 oz) blue cheese (Gorgonzola, Dolcelatte, Stilton or Cambazola), cut or crumbled into small dice
>
> 4 x 15 ml spoons (4 tablespoons) cream or crème fraîche
>
> 275 g (10 oz) quills
>
> freshly grated Parmesan

Steam or boil the courgettes or green beans in lightly salted water until *soft* and cooked but taking care to drain before they lose their sharp green colour. Drain in a colander, shaking firmly to remove excess water.

Sauté the onion, garlic and chilli (if using) in the oil or butter until the onion has softened nicely and is beginning to turn golden. Add the cooked and drained courgettes (or beans) and sage, and then sauté for another couple of minutes.

Add the blue cheese and cream or crème fraîche and sauté for another couple of minutes until the blue cheese has dissolved.

Meanwhile, cook the pasta in plenty of salted, boiling water until 'al dente', drain and return to the pan. Toss the pasta with the courgette and blue cheese sauce. Serve hot with freshly grated Parmesan on the side.

20 Quills with creamy tomato sauce, Camembert, Emmenthal and toasted pine kernels

A remarkably easy and delicious starter or main course. Good for using up ends of cheeses. Experiment with other cheeses, such as Brie, peppered Brie, Gruyère, Cambozola, and so on.

For 2 main course or 3–4 starter size helpings, use:

    1 x 15 ml spoon (1 tablespoon) olive oil
    1 clove garlic, crushed
    ½ small dried chilli, to taste, coarsely chopped
    2 anchovy fillets (optional), chopped
    225 g (8 oz) tinned chopped Italian tomatoes
    1 x 5 ml spoon (1 teaspoon) sugar
    4 x 15 ml spoons (4 tablespoons) cream (single or double)
        or crème fraîche
    25 g (1 oz) Emmenthal or Gruyère cheese, grated
    25 g (1 oz) Camembert or Brie, skinned and chopped
    25 g (1 oz) pine kernels, toasted (or substitute black olives)
    200–250 g (8–10 oz) small quills
    tarragon or basil (optional)
    freshly grated Parmesan

Sauté the garlic, chilli, anchovies (if using) and tomatoes in the olive oil with the sugar over a medium heat for about 5 or 10 minutes, or until the sauce begins to thicken into a jam-like consistency. Add the cream and the cheeses and stir over a low heat until the cheeses have melted into the sauce. If the sauce becomes a little too sticky, then just add a few table-spoons of water.

Toast the pine kernels in a non-stick pan over a low heat, stirring frequently.

Meanwhile, cook the pasta in plenty of salted, boiling water until 'al dente'. Then drain the pasta and return it to the pan with the sauce. Toss over a low heat until well heated through, and then serve on heated plates with the toasted pine kernels and chopped herbs sprinkled over the top. Serve freshly grated Parmesan on the side.

21 Rigatoni with tomato and pesto sauce and optional pine kernels, basil and/or ricotta

One of those spicy sauces which really hits the spot. If you object to 'spicy' then simply cut down or cut out the chilli and garlic.

This recipe is more or less a store cupboard standby. You can use bottled pesto or 'fresh', bought from the chilled section of the supermarket. Use more if using chilled; it's not usually as strong as the bottled. The ricotta adds a nice touch, and a very good taste combination. Serve with just one heaped spoon of ricotta on each serving.

You could substitute sun-dried tomatoes for the pine kernels, or chopped peppers in a jar, again obtainable from Marks and Spencer or Waitrose and probably other stores.

For 4–6 starter size or 2–3 main course helpings, use:

3 x 15 ml spoons (3 tablespoons) olive oil
1 small dried or fresh chilli, finely chopped
50 g (2 oz) onion, finely sliced or chopped
425 g (14 oz) tinned Italian tomatoes, coarsely chopped
2–3 cloves garlic, crushed
1 x 15 ml spoon (1 tablespoon) tomato purée
2–3 x 15 ml spoons (2–3 tablespoons) pesto sauce
    (bottled or 'chilled')
½ x 5 ml spoon (½ teaspoon) sugar
225–325 g (8–12 oz) rigatoni
fresh basil leaves (optional), torn into pieces
50 g (2 oz) pine kernels (optional)
3 heaped x 15 ml spoons (3 heaped tablespoons)
    ricotta (optional)
Parmesan cheese

Sauté the chilli and onion in the oil over a low heat until the onion softens. Add the tomatoes and simmer on a low heat, stirring frequently for about 10 minutes. Add the garlic, tomato purée, pesto sauce and sugar, and simmer for another 10 minutes or so, still on a low heat, stirring frequently. (By now the sauce should have thickened into a sort of tomato purée consistency.)

Meanwhile, cook the pasta in plenty of salted, boiling water until 'al dente'. Drain, put back into the pan with the sauce and toss over a low heat until heated through.

Serve immediately with the basil leaves and pine kernels (if using) sprinkled on top, a spoonful of ricotta (if using) on each serving and grated Parmesan on the side.

22 Twists with three cheeses, capers, lemon and cream

One of my few recipes which do *not* contain either chilli or garlic! Very fresh and tasty.

I actually made it using Marks and Spencer's 'Fiorelli', which are like frills and go under the title of 'fresh egg pasta', although they come in a cellophane packet with a 'sell-by' date two years on.

For a variation, add a can of drained tuna fish, or try out other cheeses such as Cheddar or Brie.

For 2 main course or 3–4 starter size helpings, use:

225–275 g (8–10 oz) twists
2 x 15 ml spoons (2 tablespoons) olive oil
2 x 15 ml spoons (2 tablespoons) single cream
30 g (1½ oz) Gruyère, grated
50 g (2 oz) Emmenthal, grated
25 g (1 oz) Parmesan, grated
1½ x 15 ml spoons (1½ tablespoons) lemon juice
lemon peel (about ½ lemon), pared with a sharp knife and
    then slivered
1½ x 15 ml spoons (1½ tablespoons) capers, well drained
    and chopped
chopped herbs, basil or chives or tarragon

Cook the twists in plenty of salted, boiling water until 'al dente'. Drain and put into a large frying pan with one 15 ml spoon (1 tablespoon) of the oil and toss.

Pour over the cream and the cheeses, and then stir over a low heat until the cheeses melt. Add the lemon juice and lemon peel, chopped capers, remaining spoon of oil and herbs, and stir again.

Serve hot, or warm, or even cold as a salad with extra grated Parmesan, pepper grinder and grated nutmeg (optional) on the side.

23 Tagliatelle with butter, Parmesan and pepper, and optional garlic

If you have a pasta machine, prepare the pasta according to the recipe that comes with your machine, using roughly 1 egg to 100 g (4 oz) flour, or buy fresh or chilled pasta from your local Italian delicatessen or supermarket. I've tested tagliatelle made by Waitrose, Sainsbury's and Marks and Spencer, and I would recommend them all. Or buy de Cecco or Barilla dried egg tagliatelle.

Cook the pasta in plenty of salted, boiling water until 'al dente' – remembering that fresh pasta takes much less time (about half the time) than dried pasta. But do be careful to let it cook sufficiently and don't attempt to eat it half raw. Then drain and return to the pan.

Toss with butter – about 1 or 2 x 15 ml spoons (1 or 2 tablespoons) per serving and serve with freshly ground black pepper and freshly (medium/coarsely) grated Parmesan, or else a big chunk of Parmesan with grater on the side.

With garlic

If you are a garlic fiend, then first melt the butter in a pan and gently sauté the garlic (1 or 2 cloves, crushed, per 2 servings), taking *great care* not to let it burn.

Toss with the tagliatelle and serve immediately, as above.

24 Bows with very quick and easy tomato, sun-dried tomato and pesto sauce

I keep jars of tomato purée, sun-dried tomato paste (Sacla 'Pasta-gusto' or Waitrose own) and pesto – either bottled or chilled, again from Waitrose – in the fridge. Ideal for making *really* quick (but delicious) pasta sauces. Use all three mixed together, as I have in the recipe below, or larger quantities of two, or even one of the pastes. The extra oil, garlic and chilli (as always to be adjusted if necessary 'to taste') makes all the difference.

If you are feeling energetic you could always sprinkle a couple of tablespoons of toasted pine kernels on top.

For 2 main course helpings, use:

- 1 x 15 ml spoon (1 tablespoon) olive oil
- 1 clove garlic, crushed
- ½ small dried chilli, finely chopped or crumbled
- 2 x 15 ml spoons (2 tablespoons) sun-dried tomato paste
- 2 x 15 ml spoons (2 tablespoons) tomato purée
- 1 x 15 ml spoon (1 tablespoon) pesto (bottled or chilled)
- 1 x 15 ml spoon (1 tablespoon) freshly grated Parmesan cheese
- 225 g (10 oz) bows

Whilst the pasta is cooking, sauté the crushed garlic for only about 30 seconds in the oil, in a pan or frying pan (preferably non-stick) large enough to take all the pasta. Stir in the chilli, sun-dried tomato paste, tomato purée and pesto, and stir together. Take off the heat until the pasta is ready.

Meanwhile, cook the pasta in plenty of salted, boiling water until 'al dente'. Drain, and put into the pan with the sauces, toss together over a low heat until well heated through.

Sprinkle over the Parmesan cheese, toss again and serve immediately.

More Vegetarian Dishes

- Take trouble to make sure that you are cooking with enough water. If water goes cloudy, boil up a kettle and add more boiling water.

- If you think the pasta and sauce might turn out a little dry, some people suggest draining the pasta quickly and leaving in some of the cooking water.

- Instead of serving freshly grated Parmesan, try putting a lump of Parmesan and a grater on the table so people can grate their own.

- *Always* taste the pasta before adding grated cheese. It often doesn't need it, especially any pasta with fish, and that includes anchovies.

- Always feel free to *substitute*. That's what all the best Italian cooks do – they make the sauce with whatever is in the house, the garden or available that week in the market.

- Almost all my ingredients are optional, apart from the pasta itself! Experiment with what you have and what you like, and invent your own sauces, using my recipes as a base.

- The secret of a good tomato sauce is never burning the garlic. It should always retain its white colour. If the garlic goes crispy and brown, take it out and start again!

- Adjust the chilli according to taste. It is very hard to give an accurate measurement as chillies vary. The saying is, the smaller the hotter.

- Always remember to use lots and lots of fast-boiling, lightly salted water to cook your pasta.

- If your pasta is soggy and tasteless, or continues cooking after you have drained it, here are some possible reasons:

    You've overcooked it;

    You've used an unreliable brand. Use good-quality Italian pasta, for example, de Cecco or Barilla (not Buitoni) or experiment with your local supermarket produce until you find one that works well for you.

- If your pasta is soft on the outside but still hard in the centre it could be that you are not using enough water to cook it in.

- Find a brand of pasta that you like and stock up on it. I recommend F. lli de Cecco, Barilla (not Buitoni) and Marks and Spencer dried fresh egg pasta.

- If you use a good brand of pasta and cook it correctly (with lots of salted, boiling water until it is 'al dente') it will not go mushy on you – you can even drain it, toss it with a spoonful of oil and heat it up later or the following day.

- Feel free to experiment. Be brave. Open the fridge and make a sauce with whatever falls out.

- Stock up on store cupboard standbys from the Introduction and you will always be able to dish up a meal for friends at short notice.

- If you are partial to one of the spicy tomato sauces make extra and freeze in cupfuls. Add a little extra oil after defrosting.

- Buy herbs in pots at your local supermarket and keep them on your kitchen windowsill.

- Buy pesto sauce from the chilled section of the supermarket and freeze in ice cube trays. Decant into a plastic bag and keep frozen for future use.

- I heard Delia Smith the other day on television saying, 'Life is too short to roast a red pepper.' All I can say is I disagree – totally – and I am quite a lazy cook and believe in dishes that can be prepared quickly with the minimum amount of fuss. I *don't* find roasting red peppers a hardship. It's easy-peasy and quick. Just follow my instructions.

25 Semolina and cheese gnocchi

Absolutely scrumptious! One of the all-time greats of the Italian kitchen. But be warned, it is very rich. Make sure the top is well browned and serve with a tasty mixed salad, including a crunchy green lettuce such as cos and, if possible, some rocket (arugula).

For 8 starter size or 4 main course helpings, use:

  1,150 ml (2 pints) milk
  grated nutmeg (to taste)
  salt and pepper
  225–275 g (8–10 oz) semolina
  2 eggs
  2 egg yolks
  100–125 g (4 oz) grated Parmesan cheese
  75–100 g (3 oz) grated Cheddar cheese
  25–50 g (1½ oz) butter

Add the nutmeg and seasoning to the milk and bring to the boil. Leaving the pan on a very low heat, sprinkle in the semolina, a very little at a time, stirring constantly with a wooden spoon. Take care not to add too much semolina at a time or lumps will form. (If you do get lumps, beat them out with an egg whisk, or fish them out of the pan and break them up with a fork.) Eventually the mixture will be thick enough to stand the spoon up in it. At this point, stop adding the semolina – even if you still have some left – and remove the pan from the heat. Allow to cool a little, and then stir in the eggs and egg yolks, followed by 75–100 g (3 oz) of the grated Parmesan and all the grated Cheddar.

Find a flat surface (you could use a kitchen table or sideboard, or baking trays) where the gnocchi can lie undisturbed for a few hours, or even overnight. Spread out a large piece of foil, oil it, and spread the gnocchi mixture over it about 1 cm (½ inch) thick. Leave for several hours, and then cut out little rounds using a pastry cutter or tumbler, just as if you were making biscuits. Grease a shallow ovenproof dish and spread the rounds across the bottom so that they overlap like a spread deck of cards. Melt the butter, pour over the gnocchi, and sprinkle the remaining Parmesan cheese on top. Bake in a medium oven (190°C/375°F/gas mark 5) for 20–30 minutes until well browned on top. (If necessary, brown for a few minutes under a hot grill.)

Serve very hot.

26 Penne primavera

This dish is an improvisation on a well-known Italian theme, pasta primavera. The ingredients came from a local supermarket where I bought whatever fresh vegetables caught my eye. The dish can be eaten hot or cold.

As with most of my pasta recipes, I recommend that you, too, improvise a little if you feel like it. You could substitute various other vegetables including fennel, mushrooms, fresh peas, cauliflower, asparagus, red pepper – and particularly courgettes.

For 4 main course helpings, use:

100–125 g (4 oz) broccoli, broken into small pieces
100–125 g (4 oz) small French beans, cut into 5 cm
  (2 inch) lengths
100–125 g (4 oz) carrots, julienned or cut into thin sticks
100–125 g (4 oz) mange-tout peas (if available)
2 x 15 ml spoons (2 tablespoons) fresh, chopped herbs
  or ½ x 15 ml spoon (½ tablespoon) dried herbs
450 g (1 lb) quills

For the vinaigrette
9 x 15 ml spoons (9 tablespoons) olive oil
3 x 15 ml spoons (3 tablespoons) wine or balsamic vinegar
2 x 5 ml spoons (2 teaspoons) French or German mustard
  or 1 x 5 ml spoon (1 teaspoon) English mustard
1 x 5 ml spoon (1 teaspoon) caster sugar
freshly grated nutmeg (optional)
1 clove garlic, crushed (optional)
salt and pepper

Steam the vegetables for 2–4 minutes until slightly softened but still brightly coloured and crisp. If you do not possess a steamer, then boil the vegetables one at a time for just 1–2 minutes, using a slotted spoon to remove them so that you can re-use the boiling water. Drain, and put all the vegetables into a large bowl. Using a fork, beat the vinaigrette ingredients together in a cup and pour over the vegetables. Add fresh or dried herbs. Mix well.

Meanwhile, cook the pasta in salted, boiling water until 'al dente'. Drain, and mix into the bowl of vegetables and vinaigrette.

Serve either hot or cold.

27 Spinach lasagne

A very handy dish, comparatively light and simple in flavours and preparation. This recipe comes from my first book, *Pastability*.

For 6 main course helpings, use:

For the spinach filling
900–925 g (2 lb) spinach
25–50 g (1½ oz) butter
2 cloves garlic, crushed
325–350 g (12 oz) cottage cheese
2 egg yolks
grated rind of 1 large lemon (or 1½ small lemons)
¾ x 5 ml spoon (¾ teaspoon) grated nutmeg (to taste)
100–125 g (4 oz) grated Cheddar cheese
salt and pepper

For the béchamel sauce
25–50 g (1½ oz) butter
25–50 g (1½ oz) flour
575 ml (1 pint) milk
½ x 5 ml spoon (½ teaspoon) mustard powder

Additional ingredients
salt and pepper
450 g (1 lb) lasagne
175 g (6 oz) grated Cheddar cheese

If you are using frozen spinach, defrost it in a little boiling, salted water. Strain, pushing the spinach against the strainer or colander to remove as much liquid as possible. If the spinach is fresh, cook it in a very little milk or water, strain, and chop coarsely.

Melt the butter in the bottom of a large saucepan on a very low heat. Add the garlic, and almost immediately add the spinach, sautéing for a few minutes on the low heat. Put to one side. Mix together the cottage cheese, egg yolks, lemon rind, nutmeg, Cheddar cheese and seasoning, and add to the cooled spinach. Mix all the ingredients together well.

Make a béchamel sauce with the ingredients stated, following the instructions on page 224.

Cook the lasagne as instructed on page 6.

Take a fairly shallow ovenproof dish (7.5–10 cm/3–4 inches deep) and butter it well. Spread a thin layer of the spinach mixture on the bottom of the dish. Spread a couple of large spoonfuls of béchamel sauce over it, then add some grated cheese and seasoning. Follow with a layer of lasagne, overlapping the edges slightly. Repeat the process until you run out of ingredients, ending with some béchamel sauce on top of the last layer of lasagne, and a generous sprinkling of Cheddar cheese.

Cover the dish with foil, and bake in a fairly hot oven (200°C/400°F/gas mark 6) for 1–1½ hours. Remove the foil for the last 15–20 minutes to allow the cheese topping to brown.

28 Pasta bake

This recipe was given to me by Louise Arthur – our charming and long-suffering assistant. Louise is also a professional French horn player. She works for us all day and plays the horn all night. God knows when she sleeps!

Louise helped enormously with this book, typing out most of the recipes – deciphering my impossible hieroglyphics and scribbled corrections and enacting wizardry on the computer in order to present the publisher with the book 'on disk', as is the requirement of publishers nowadays.

For 4 main course helpings, use:

    1 small onion, finely chopped
    50 g (2 oz) butter
    115 g (4 oz) mushrooms, chopped
    75 g (3 oz) parsley, finely chopped
    275 ml (½ pint) soured cream or crème fraîche
    225 g (8 oz) tagliatelle
    115 g (4 oz) Mozzarella cheese
    90 g (3 oz) Parmesan cheese

Sauté the onion in the butter until translucent. Add the mushrooms and parsley and cook until soft. Stir in the soured cream. Put aside.

Meanwhile, cook the pasta in plenty of salted, boiling water until 'al dente'. Drain.

Butter an ovenproof dish. Using half the ingredients, put in a layer of tagliatelle, then a layer of the cream sauce and then a layer of the cheeses. Repeat, using the other half of the ingredients, ending up with the cheese on top.

Bake in a preheated oven (200°C/400°F/gas mark 6) for 20 minutes or until the cheese has melted and bubbles on the top.

Serve immediately.

29 The Actors' Centre lentil and spinach lasagne

Actors are by nature gregarious and friendly creatures who like to be 'where the action is'. The Actors' Centre fulfils a very necessary function, providing us Thespians who *don't* like pubs with a place to go, where we can study plays and techniques, acquire new skills, and talk to each other. The Centre has always made a point of providing delicious and healthy food at extremely reasonable prices.

This lasagne recipe was given to me a couple of years ago by their chef at that time, Elaine Fradley, and is surprisingly light and fresh.

For 4 main course helpings, use:

1 large onion (175 g/6 oz) finely sliced or chopped
1 x 15 ml spoon (1 tablespoon) butter
   and a further 50 g (2 oz) butter
225 g (8 oz) continental lentils
2 bay leaves
850 ml (1½ pints) water
675 g (1½ lb) spinach, fresh or frozen
zest of one lemon, grated
4 x 15 ml spoons (4 tablespoons) lemon juice
grated nutmeg
salt and pepper
2 cloves garlic, crushed
1 x 15 ml spoon (1 tablespoon) parsley, finely chopped
   or 1 x 15 ml spoon (1 tablespoon) fresh coriander,
   finely chopped
4 x 15 ml spoons (4 tablespoons) white wine (optional)
450 g (1 lb) soft white cheese (curd, cottage, 'quark' or
   fromage frais)
2 eggs
225 g (8 oz) lasagne
75–100 g (3 oz) cheese, grated (strong Cheddar,
   Emmenthal or Gruyère)

Sauté half the sliced or chopped onion in the spoonful of butter until translucent and softened. Add the lentils, bay leaves and water and simmer for 30–40 minutes, until the lentils are softened.

Wash the spinach (if using fresh). Whether using fresh or frozen, cook on a low flame with no extra water, just 25 g (1 oz) of butter, in a covered pan for 7 minutes (or until defrosted). Add the grated zest of lemon, and 1 x 15 ml spoon (1 tablespoon) of lemon juice. Season with nutmeg, salt and pepper to taste.

Sauté the garlic and the rest of the onion in 25 g (1 oz) of the butter. Add the lentils, parsley or coriander, wine and the remaining 3 x 15 ml spoons (3 tablespoons) of lemon juice. Beat together the soft cheese and eggs and season.

Cook the lasagne as directed on page 6.

Grease a large, shallow ovenproof dish. Put in half the lentil mixture, half the spinach, one third of the egg and soft cheese mixture, and a light sprinkling of the grated cheese. Follow this with a layer of lasagne. Repeat the layers, ending with the remaining cheese mixture and a good sprinkling of grated cheese.

Bake in a preheated oven (200°C/400°F/gas mark 6) for about 45 minutes, or until golden brown.

30 Twists with red and yellow roast peppers, caramelised onions and goat's cheese (or feta)

This is the sort of dish that's served in smart 'Californian cuisine' restaurants as a starter, with possibly a few arugula (rocket) leaves scattered around for good measure. It's quite scrumptious and very attractive in appearance with the contrasting colours of the peppers, beans, cheese and pine kernels. If you don't like goat's cheese or feta you can make this dish substituting a cream cheese, or even a mild, blue-veined cream cheese such as Cambozola.

For 2 main course or 4 starter size helpings, use:

- 1 medium to large red pepper
- 1 medium to large yellow pepper
- 3 x 15 ml spoons (3 tablespoons) olive oil
- 100 g (4 oz) green beans (chopped into 2 cm /1 inch lengths) and blanched
- 1 medium sized (125 g/4 oz) onion, quartered and then coarsely chopped
- 1 small chilli (fresh or dried) to taste, finely chopped
- 1 x 5 ml spoon (1 teaspoon) sugar
- 1–2 cloves garlic, crushed
- 4 tinned anchovy fillets, coarsely chopped (optional)
- ½ x 15 ml spoon (½ tablespoon) balsamic vinegar
- 225 g (8 oz) twists
- 50 g (2 oz) goat's cheese (or feta), coarsely chopped
- 2 x 15 ml spoons (2 tablespoons) pine kernels (lightly toasted in a non-stick pan)
- 2 x 15 ml spoons (2 tablespoons) chopped fresh green herbs (when available) such as basil or parsley.

Place the whole peppers on the grill pan (removing the rack if necessary), with the peppers almost touching the heating element, and grill on a high heat on all four sides until the peppers turn completely black. Allow to cool and then peel off the black, burnt skin. Cut into halves, remove the stalk and seeds and then slice the slightly cooked and softened pepper into strips and lay out on a plate. Dribble a spoonful or so of the oil over the strips, and leave for 10 minutes or whilst you organize the rest of the ingredients.

Steam or lightly boil the green beans for a few minutes only, until just cooked but still crunchy and green. (Or throw them into the boiling pasta water before using for cooking the pasta, removing the beans with a slotted spoon when cooked.) Put aside.

Sauté the onion with the chopped chilli in 2 x 15 ml spoons (2 tablespoons) of the olive oil until the onion becomes translucent and begins to turn golden. Add the sugar, turn up the heat and continue to sauté for another minute or two to caramelise the onion. Turn the heat back down low, and add the crushed garlic, anchovies (if using), balsamic vinegar, sliced roasted red peppers and blanched beans. Stir together over a low heat for a couple of minutes and then leave aside in the pan until the pasta is ready.

Meanwhile, cook the pasta in plenty of salted, boiling water until 'al dente', drain, and return to the pan with the sauce.

Toss the sauce and pasta with the chopped cheese in the pan until well heated through. At the last moment before serving, sprinkle over the toasted pine kernels and freshly chopped herbs (if using).

31 Carrot, courgette, leek and mushroom lasagne

This dish is delicious – fresh but substantial. Feel free to experiment with ingredients; for example, try out other British cheeses rather than the Cheddar, such as Cheshire, Wensleydale and so on, or substitute broccoli for the leeks or courgettes.

For 6 main course helpings, use:

For the carrot and leek filling
25 g (1 oz) butter
2 x 15 ml spoons (2 tablespoons) olive oil
100–125 g (4 oz) onion, finely sliced
1 clove garlic, crushed
225 g (8 oz) leeks, finely sliced
450 g (1 lb) carrots, finely sliced or chopped
3 x 15 ml spoons (3 tablespoons) fruit juice (apple or orange)

For the courgette and mushroom filling
25 g (1 oz) butter
2 x 15 ml spoons (2 tablespoons) olive oil
100–125 g (4 oz) onion, finely sliced
1 clove garlic, crushed
325–350 g (12 oz) mushrooms, sliced
325–350 g (12 oz) courgettes, finely sliced

For the béchamel sauce
25 g (1 oz) butter
25 g (1 oz) flour
575 ml (1 pint) milk
1 x 5 ml spoon (1 teaspoon) dry mustard powder

Additional ingredients
300–500 g (11–18 oz) lasagne
225 g (8 oz) grated Cheddar cheese
150 ml (¼ pint) single cream
100–125 g (4 oz) shelled walnuts

Take 2 large saucepans with lids and start cooking the carrot and courgette fillings simultaneously. In each pan sauté the onion and garlic in the oil and butter on a very low heat, removing the lid to stir occasionally, until the onion is quite mushy. (Alternatively, leave them both in the oven at 140°C/275°F/gas mark 1 for 30 minutes, stirring occasionally.)

Add the sliced mushrooms to one of the pans, stirring well over a low heat to allow them to absorb the juices. After 2–3 minutes add the courgettes. Replace the lid and leave over a low heat, stirring occasionally, for about 10 minutes (if it seems too dry, add a little water.)

Add the leeks to the other pan of onion mixture, stirring well over a gentle heat for a few minutes. Then add the carrots and fruit juice. Leave to cook on a low flame, covered, for a further 10 minutes, stirring occasionally.

Make a thin béchamel sauce, following the instructions on page 224.

Cook the lasagne, following the instructions on page 6.

Take a flat, ovenproof dish, 7.5–10 cm (3–4 inches) deep, and butter it well. (I use an earthenware oval dish about 38 cm [15 inches] x 25 cm [10 inches] x 6 cm [2½ inches]). Spread a thin layer of the carrot filling over the bottom so that it barely hides the base. Spread over it a couple of tablespoons of béchamel sauce, sprinkle on some Cheddar cheese, and then lay a layer of lasagne with the strips just overlapping at the edges. Then spread a layer each of the courgette filling, béchamel and cheese, followed by a layer of lasagne. Continue this way until all the ingredients are used up (I aim for about 2 layers of each filling), ending with a layer of lasagne on which you spread a fairly generous dollop of béchamel sauce.

Pour the cream all over the top, and sprinkle on the nuts and a handful of grated cheese. Cover with foil so that the pasta will absorb some of the juices, and cook in a hot oven (200°C/400°F/gas mark 6) for 1–1½ hours, depending on when you are ready to eat, removing the foil for the last 15–30 minutes to allow the dish to brown.

32 Spaghetti with tomatoes, red pepper, olives and Mozzarella cheese

The roast red pepper gives this dish a pleasant tangy flavour which contrasts well with the mildness and chewy quality of the cheese. Served with a green salad this makes an excellent supper dish. It looks fresh and pretty but is also substantial, and it is good enough to serve even on a special occasion.

For 2 main course helpings, use:

  1 red pepper (medium size)
  2 x 15 ml spoons (2 tablespoons) olive oil
  salt and pepper
  75–100 g (3 oz) onion, finely sliced
  8 olives (green or black), pitted and chopped
  ½ wine glass (50 ml/2 fl oz) red or white wine (optional)
  175 g (6 oz) tomatoes, skinned and coarsely chopped (or substitute tinned tomatoes)
  ½ x 5 ml spoon (½ teaspoon) dried thyme
  225 g (8 oz) spaghetti
  15 g (½ oz) butter
  50 g (2 oz) Mozzarella cheese (or another mild, hard cheese), cut into small pieces

Place the whole red pepper on the grill pan, with the pepper nearly touching the heating element, and grill under a high heat. (Most of the skin will turn black but will peel off to reveal an unburnt, delicious pepper underneath.) Remove from the grill, cool slightly and peel, then cut the peeled pepper into strips and lay on a plate. Dribble ½ x 15 ml spoon (½ tablespoon) of the olive oil over the strips, and sprinkle with a little salt and pepper. Leave for a few minutes, then slice into smaller pieces.

Sauté the onion in the remaining olive oil for a few minutes until softened and translucent. Add the chopped olives and the grilled red pepper. Stir in the wine (if using), tomatoes and the thyme. Simmer on a low heat with the lid on for 7–8 minutes, stirring occasionally and adding a little water (from the pasta pot) if the sauce is getting at all dry or is sticking to the bottom of the pan. Season.

Meanwhile, cook the pasta in plenty of salted, boiling water until 'al dente'. Drain and put back into the pan over a low heat. Stir in the butter, the sauce and the Mozzarella cheese.

Serve immediately the cheese starts to melt.

33 Twists with pumpkin (or butternut squash), herbs and pine nuts

I first experienced pasta with a pumpkin sauce in a small Italian restaurant in Perth on the west coast of Australia. They served the 'Spaghetti with Pumpkin and Garlic' from within a hollowed-out pumpkin – quite a good idea for Hallowe'en. Both pumpkin and butternut squash have a certain natural sweetness which you either like or don't like. I love it.

You can make an exquisite version of this pasta substituting sweet potatoes (yams) (preferably the ones with the orange flesh), baked until soft, peeled and cut into chunks.

For 3–4 main course or 6 starter size helpings, use:

> 900 g (2 lb) pumpkin or butternut squash
> 2 x 15 ml spoons (2 tablespoons) olive oil
> 1 x 15 ml spoon (1 tablespoon) butter
> 100 g (4 oz) onion, chopped
> 2 cloves garlic, crushed
> ½ dried chilli, finely chopped (to taste)
> 400–500 g (14–18 oz) twists
> 3 x 15 ml spoons (3 tablespoons) Greek yoghurt (or crème fraîche) (optional)
> salt and pepper
> 2 x 15 ml spoons (2 heaped tablespoons) fresh green herbs (chives, tarragon or basil) finely chopped
> 25 g (1 oz) toasted pine kernels (or chopped walnuts)
> ground nutmeg or cayenne pepper (optional) on the side

Cut the pumpkin or squash into 2-inch wedges, place on a baking tray and bake in a hot oven (200°C/400°F/gas mark 6) for about an hour or until fairly soft. Allow to cool for a few minutes, and then peel off the skin and cut into chunks the size of large sugar lumps. Sauté the onion over a low heat with the two cloves of crushed garlic and the half chilli in one tablespoon (1 x 15 ml spoon) of the oil and all the butter, until the onion is translucent and beginning to turn golden. Throw in the pumpkin (or squash) and continue to gently fry until the pumpkin has mixed with the onions, and absorbed the juices. Put aside.

Meanwhile, cook the pasta in plenty of salted, boiling water until 'al dente'. Scoop out about a cup of the salted water in which the pasta was cooked and reserve. Then drain the pasta and return it to the pan, pouring over and tossing together with the remaining spoon of olive oil.

Heat the pumpkin and onion sauce through, adding the yoghurt or crème fraîche (if using), and then toss together with the pasta. Season to taste. If the pasta seems a little dry and sticky for your taste, add a bit of the reserved cooking liquid (or even a little fresh single cream if you prefer).

Serve hot with the herbs and toasted pine kernels sprinkled on top. Serve Parmesan on the side if you must, but please encourage your guests to taste the pasta first to decide whether or not it really needs the addition of cheese.

34 Linguini (or spaghetti) with courgettes, aubergine, roasted red peppers and pumpkin (or butternut squash)

A very pretty dish with the red of the pepper, black of the aubergine, green courgette and orange pumpkin (or squash) against the creamy colour of the pasta. Each mouthful brings a different flavour. I would recommend serving it as a starter.

For 4 main course or 6–8 starter size helpings, use:

450 g (1 lb) pumpkin or butternut squash
4 x 15 ml spoons (4 tablespoons) olive oil
½ tablespoon (½ x 15 ml spoon) butter
75 g (3 oz) onion, chopped
3 cloves garlic, peeled and crushed
1 (small) dried chilli, finely chopped (to taste)
160 g (6 oz) aubergine
1 medium red pepper
160 g (6 oz) courgettes, sliced
400–500 g (14–18 oz) linguini or spaghetti
3 x 15 ml spoons (3 tablespoons) Greek yoghurt
   (or crème fraîche) (optional)
2 x 15 ml spoons (2 heaped tablespoons) fresh green herbs
   (chives, tarragon or basil), finely chopped
25 g (1 oz) toasted pine kernels (or chopped walnuts)
ground nutmeg or cayenne pepper (optional) on the side.

Cut the pumpkin or squash into 2-inch wedges, place on a baking tray and bake in a hot oven (200°C/400°F/gas mark 6) for about an hour or until fairly soft. Allow to cool for a few minutes, and then peel off the skin and cut into chunks the size of large sugar lumps. Sauté the onion over a low heat with two of the cloves of crushed garlic and half the chilli in 1 x 15 ml spoon (1 tablespoon) of the oil and all the butter, until the onion is translucent and beginning to turn golden. Throw in the pumpkin (or squash) and continue to fry gently until the pumpkin has mixed with the onions, and absorbed the juices. Put aside.

Cut the aubergine into thick slices and leave sprinkled with salt on a kitchen towel to drain. After 10 or 15 minutes turn the slices, and leave them for another 10 minutes. Chop them coarsely.

Place the whole red pepper on the grill pan, with the pepper nearly touching the heating element, and grill under a high heat. (Most of the skin will turn black but will peel off to reveal an unburnt, delicious pepper underneath.) Remove from the grill, cool slightly and peel, then cut the peeled pepper into strips and lay on a plate. Dribble ½ x 15 ml spoon (½ tablespoon) of the olive oil over the strips, and sprinkle with a little salt and pepper. Leave for a few minutes, then slice into smaller pieces.

Sauté the sliced courgettes and the aubergine in the remaining oil over a medium heat, until the aubergine has softened and darkened and half the courgette has started to turn golden and pale brown. Add the roasted red pepper strips, and the cooled pumpkin (or squash) mixture and continue to fry gently for a few moments until well mixed and heated through.

Meanwhile, cook the pasta in plenty of salted, boiling water until 'al dente'. Scoop out about a cup of the salted water in which the pasta was cooked and reserve. Then drain the pasta and return it to the pan. Add the sauce and toss together with the yoghurt (or crème fraîche) (if using) and half the herbs over a low flame until the pasta is nice and hot and well integrated with the sauce, adding a little of the reserved cooking water if the pasta seems too dry and sticky. Serve immediately with the remaining herbs and toasted pine kernels sprinkled on top. There's no need to serve grated cheese with this dish.

35 Tagliatelle (or quills) with roast mixed vegetables

This is a very fashionable dish; roast vegetables seem to be all the rage these days. It certainly looks and tastes good. Toasted pine kernels are the flavour of the year, and rightly so as they are delicious and easy to prepare. However, if you are by now sick of the sight of them, leave them out or use another nut, for example, broken walnuts, pecan nuts or toasted sunflower or pumpkin seeds.

For 2 main course or 4 starter size helpings, use:

175 g (6 oz) cherry or vine tomatoes
225 g (8 oz) aubergine
olive oil
2 x 5 ml spoons (2 teaspoons) dried oregano, or substitute thyme
175 g (6 oz) red peppers
175 g (6 oz) small onions (or medium size, cut into quarters)
several large garlic cloves, peeled, and 1 crushed
225 g (8 oz) peeled sweet potato or parsnip, peeled and parboiled
1 dried chilli (optional)
225 g (8 oz) tagliatelle or quills
50 g (2 oz) toasted pine kernels (optional)

Slice the cherry tomatoes into halves. Lay them on a large baking tray covered with foil, sprinkle over a little oil and oregano and bake in the oven on a very low temperature (150°C/300°F/gas mark 2) for 45 minutes.

Cut the aubergine into thick slices and leave sprinkled with salt on a kitchen towel to drain. After 10 or 15 minutes turn the slices, and leave them for another 10 minutes. Chop them coarsely.

Meanwhile, slice the red peppers, prepare the onions, garlic cloves and sweet potato or parsnip as directed, chop into chunks and toss in olive oil with the 1 crushed garlic clove and remaining herbs and aubergine (and chilli, if using) until every surface is coated. Spread the vegetables with the partially cooked tomatoes on the baking tray and bake as before for another 2 hours.

Meanwhile, cook the pasta in plenty of salted, boiling water until 'al dente'. Drain and toss with a couple of table-spoons of olive oil (and extra chilli and garlic if you are addicted to really spicy food). Serve separately on each plate with the roasted vegetables on top of the pasta, the toasted pine kernels and more herbs, according to taste, on top of the vegetables.

36 Quills with spicy Indian tomato sauce, tofu and sesame seeds

It goes without saying that you must like spicy Indian food and/or curries to enjoy this dish.

For 3–4 main course helpings, use:

1 x 15 ml spoon (1 tablespoon) vegetable oil
2 x 15 ml spoons (2 tablespoons) butter
100 g (4 oz) onion, finely sliced or chopped
3 cloves garlic, chopped or crushed
1 x 15 ml spoon (1 tablespoon) ginger root, finely chopped or grated
¼ x 5 ml spoon (¼ teaspoon) turmeric
1 x 5 ml spoon (1 teaspoon) ground coriander
1 x 5 ml spoon (1 teaspoon) ground cumin
¼ x 5 ml spoon (¼ teaspoon) chilli powder
150 g (5 oz) tinned tomatoes, chopped
½ x 15 ml spoon (½ tablespoon) tomato purée (generous)
200 ml (7½ fl oz) water
1 x 5 ml spoon (1 teaspoon) sugar
pinch of salt
300 g (12 oz) bean curd/tofu, firm and cut into cubes
1 x 15 ml spoon (1 tablespoon) sesame seed oil (or vegetable oil)
2 x 15 ml spoons (2 tablespoons) toasted sesame seeds
300–450 g (12–16 oz) quills
3 x 15 ml spoons (3 tablespoons) cream
chopped coriander leaves

Stir-fry the onion, garlic and ginger in the vegetable oil and butter over a medium heat for 3 or 4 minutes, or until the onion is well softened and beginning to turn golden. Turn the heat low. Add the spices and chilli and stir together for another minute or so, before adding the chopped tinned tomatoes, the tomato purée, the water, sugar and salt. Stir together, cover and simmer for about 15 minutes, stirring occasionally.

Meanwhile, cut the tofu into chunks, about 2.5 cm (1 inch) square and 2 cm (¾ inch) deep, and fry in the sesame seed (or vegetable) oil with one of the tablespoons of toasted sesame seeds until golden brown.

Cook the pasta in plenty of salted, boiling water until 'al dente'. Then drain the pasta and return it to the pan.

Add the cream and half the coriander leaves to the tomato sauce. Stir together. Pour over the pasta and then toss together over a low flame until well mixed and heated through.

Serve with the fried tofu, with the remaining sesame seeds and chopped coriander sprinkled on top.

37 Tagliatelle with creamy pesto and basil

Very simple and very delicious, and particularly good on home-made pasta. Use either pesto from a jar or pesto from the chilled section of your local supermarket. I buy chilled pesto from Waitrose and would highly recommend it.

For 3–4 starter size or 2 main course helpings, use:

25 g (1 oz) pine kernels, toasted (optional)
4 x 15 ml spoons (4 tablespoons) pesto sauce
4 x 15 ml spoons (4 tablespoons) cream or crème fraîche
225 g (8 oz) tagliatelle (dried) *or* 300 g (12 oz) fresh
12 leaves basil (optional), torn into small pieces
freshly grated Parmesan

Dry-fry the pine kernels in a non-stick pan over a low heat, stirring frequently until lightly toasted.

Mix the pesto and cream together, place in a pan and heat through over a low heat.

Meanwhile, cook the pasta in plenty of salted, boiling water until 'al dente', drain and return to the pan. Toss together with the sauce and serve piping hot with the basil and pine kernels (if using) sprinkled over the top. Serve Parmesan on the side.

38 Courgette, mushroom, red pepper and sweet potato lasagne with pesto sauce and pine kernels

I sampled this very delicious and unusual dish at the Grissini restaurant in the Hyatt hotel in Hong Kong, and the chef, Josef Budde, very kindly sent me the recipe. The original recipe was just courgette (and other green vegetables) filling. I added the sweet potato and pumpkin mixture for fun (and colour). Again, feel free to experiment. You could make the lasagne doubling the courgette filling and leaving out the pumpkin and potato.

If you are using parsnips and carrots, sauté first the parsnips with a little orange juice, butter and sugar, and then the carrot with the same.

For 6 main course helpings, use:

For the pepper, sweet potato and pumpkin mix
3 large peppers (red or yellow or mixed)
325 g (12 oz) sweet potato
325 g (12 oz) pumpkin, kabobosch or yams,
    or substitute parsnips and carrots
4 x 15 ml spoons (4 tablespoons) olive oil

For the mushroom, courgette and peas mix
100 g (4 oz) onion, chopped
2 cloves garlic, crushed
1 dried chilli, chopped
175 g (6 oz) mushrooms
325 g (12 oz) courgettes, finely sliced
225 g (8 oz) peas
1 x 15 ml spoon (1 tablespoon) butter

For the béchamel sauce
35 g (1½ oz) butter
35 g (1½ oz) flour
1 pint milk

1 x 5 ml spoon (1 teaspoon) mustard powder
pinch of grated nutmeg

For the pesto sauce
275 g (10 oz) bottled pesto sauce
4 x 15 ml spoons (4 tablespoons) olive oil
4 cloves garlic, crushed (optional)
4 x 15 ml spoons (4 tablespoons) white wine or vermouth

Additional ingredients
275–325 g (10–12 oz) lasagne
35 g (1½ oz) toasted pine nuts
50 g (2 oz) Parmesan cheese, coarsely grated

Place the whole peppers on the grill pan (removing the rack if necessary), with the peppers almost touching the heating element, and grill on a high heat on all four sides until the peppers turn completely black. Allow to cool and then peel off the black burnt skin. Cut into halves, remove the stalk and seeds and then slice the slightly cooked and softened pepper into strips and lay out on a plate. Dribble a spoonful or so of the oil over the strips and put aside.

Roast the sweet potatoes and the pumpkin or kabobosch, cut into wedges and put on a baking tray in a medium oven (190°C/375°F/gas mark 5) for about 1¼ to 1½ hours. Allow to cool, peel and coarsely chop.

Sauté the onion, garlic and chilli in 3 x 15 ml spoons (3 tablespoons) of the olive oil until the onion has turned translucent. Add the mushrooms, cover and turn up the heat for a couple of minutes (the mushrooms will then produce their own juices). Uncover, stir and then add the courgettes and sauté for another 7 or 8 minutes until the courgettes soften. Add the peas and the 15 ml spoon (1 tablespoon) butter and cook for another 2 or 3 minutes. Remove from the heat and put aside until time to layer into the lasagne.

Make the béchamel sauce with the ingredients listed, according to recipe 1 or 2 on page 224.

Meanwhile, cook the lasagne as instructed on page 6.

Take a flat, ovenproof dish, 7½–10 cm (3–4 inches) deep,

and butter it well. Spread a thin layer of the roast peppers, sweet potato and pumpkin mixture over the bottom so that it barely hides the base. Spread over this a couple of table-spoons of béchamel sauce, and then lay a layer of lasagne with the strips just overlapping at the edges. Spread over it a thin layer of the mushroom, courgette and peas mixture, béchamel and a layer of lasagne. Continue this way until all the ingredients are used up (I aim for about 2 layers of each filling), ending with a layer of lasagne on which you spread a fairly generous dollop of béchamel sauce.

Cover with foil so that the pasta will absorb some of the juices, and cook in a hot oven (200°C/400°F/gas mark 6) for 1–1½ hours, depending on when you are ready to eat, removing the foil for the last 15–30 minutes to allow the dish to brown.

Combine the ingredients for the pesto sauce in a pan and heat over a low flame, stirring gently until heated through. Dry-fry the pine kernels over a low heat in a non-stick pan, turning almost continuously with a wooden spoon.

Divide the lasagne into servings, remove with a fish slice and serve on heated plates in individual portions with a spoon of the pesto sauce and pine kernels sprinkled over each portion, and Parmesan served on the side.

39 Tagliatelle with dried and fresh mushrooms and cream

I make this dish frequently and am always surprised by how absolutely delicious it is.

Dried mushrooms can be found in little tinfoil or cellophane packets in good delicatessens and some supermarkets. Although they *are* expensive, you will only need one small packet for this recipe. They have an interesting, rich, slightly sweet flavour which combines well with cream. I find the sauce goes particularly well with an egg pasta such as tagliatelle, and I sometimes make this dish with (bought) fresh pasta.

Cater for second helpings; there will be plenty of requests!

For 6 starter size helpings, use:

15 g (½ oz) dried mushrooms
25–50 g (1½ oz) butter
1 clove garlic, crushed
50 g (2 oz) onion, finely chopped
325–350 g (12 oz) fresh mushrooms, finely sliced
150 ml/5 fl oz (¼ pint) double cream
325–350 g (12 oz) tagliatelle
grated cheese (optional)
salt and pepper

Soak the dried mushrooms in 425 ml/15 fl oz (¾ pint) warm water for 20–30 minutes until softened. Strain, reserving some of the liquid, and pat dry with kitchen paper. Then chop into small pieces.

Sauté the garlic and onion in the butter until the onion begins to soften, then add the porcini and continue to sauté for a few minutes on a low heat, taking care not to let the ingredients burn. Add 3 x 15 ml spoons (3 tablespoons) of the reserved porcini liquid, then stir in the fresh mushrooms. Place the lid on the pan and turn up the heat to allow the mushrooms to produce their juices. After a couple of minutes, stir with a wooden spoon and then continue cooking until the mushrooms are well softened. Pour in the cream and heat through, seasoning to taste. The sauce should be reheated just before adding to the cooked pasta.

Cook the pasta in plenty of salted, boiling water. Drain when 'al dente' and put into a preheated serving dish or back into the pan. Stir in a knob of butter with a wooden spoon and then pour the sauce over the pasta.

Serve with grated cheese on the side if desired, though personally I prefer it without.

40 Aubergine, tomato and cheese mould ('sformata') with pesto sauce and toasted pine kernels

A sort of 'cake' made with pasta with a covering of aubergine slices. It's a good way of making a pasta dish look rather special if you are entertaining.

Being very health- and weight-conscious, I have tried to keep oil and butter to a minimum in my books. However delicious, they are both 100 calories a tablespoon (15 ml spoon). What I hate about aubergines is that they drink up so much oil, and thus become calorific. The clever thing about this dish though is that you are getting maximum mileage from your aubergine slices, as they are *all* visible!

An optional extra would be to throw into the mixture 75 g (3 oz) sun-dried tomatoes, coarsely chopped.

For *approximately* 4 main course helpings, use:

    1 large or two medium-sized aubergines
    olive oil
    1 clove garlic, crushed
    225 g (8 oz) medium-sized macaroni, shells or quills

For the béchamel sauce
    25 g (1 oz) butter
    25 g (1 oz) flour
    575 ml (1 pint) milk (full cream or semi-skimmed)
    50 g (2 oz) Parmesan *or* 75 g (3 oz) Ementhal or Cheddar
      cheese, coarsely grated
    1 x 5 ml spoon (1 teaspoon) mustard powder
    grated nutmeg (to taste)
    salt and pepper

For the tomato sauce
    1 x 15 ml spoon (1 tablespoon) olive oil
    1 or 2 cloves garlic, crushed

1 dried chilli, crumbled (optional)
400 g (14 oz) tinned tomatoes, coarsely chopped
1 x 15 ml spoon (1 tablespoon) tomato purée
1 x 5 ml spoon (1 teaspoon) dried oregano
1 x 5 ml spoon (1 teaspoon) sugar

For the pesto sauce

2 x 15 ml spoons (2 tablespoons) olive oil
2 x 15 ml spoons (2 tablespoons) pesto sauce
   (bottled or chilled)
1 clove garlic, crushed

Additional ingredients

50 g (2 oz) Parmesan cheese, grated (*or* substitute
   Cheshire or Emmenthal)
50 g (2 oz) pine kernels

Slice the aubergine into quite *thin* slices and leave to drain on some kitchen roll for half an hour, turning over after 15 minutes.

Cook the béchamel sauce as directed on page 224, using the simpler method (2). Stir in the cheese and the mustard powder, and season to taste.

Fry the aubergine slices in the oil with the clove of crushed garlic until both sides are golden brown. Leave to drain on some kitchen roll.

To make the tomato sauce, sauté the garlic and chilli in the oil for a minute or so, taking care not to burn it. Add the tomatoes, tomato purée, sugar and herbs and simmer for 15 to 20 minutes.

Meanwhile, cook the pasta in plenty of salted, boiling water until 'al dente' (if anything, a fraction undercooked – if it is borderline overcooked at this stage then it will be horren-dously mushy and white at the final stage). Drain and put back in the pan with a little oil or butter.

Take an ovenproof dish (I use a round Pyrex bowl which has gently sloping sides). Line the base and sides with the slices of aubergine, overlapping them a little.

Pour the béchamel sauce over the drained pasta and mix

together. Put a layer of the pasta and béchamel into the bottom of the ovenproof dish, over the aubergines. Spread over a thin layer of tomato sauce, sprinkle on a few toasted pine kernels and a little grated Parmesan cheese, another layer of pasta with béchamel, then tomato, and so on until you run out of ingredients. Sprinkle over any remaining cheese, but keep the remaining toasted pine kernels. Bake in a moderate oven (190°C/375°F/gas mark 5) for about half an hour.

Mix the pesto sauce with the oil and garlic.

When the dish is ready, remove from the oven and turn out onto a plate. Sprinkle the remaining toasted pine kernels over the top and serve with a 10 ml spoon (dessertspoon) of the pesto sauce on each helping.

41 Spinach cannelloni

Here is my version of a very traditional Italian dish. It's a bit of a
bore stuffing those tubes with the ingredients, but you could
always use lasagne leaves and roll them up with the stuffing in the
middle. You can even make this dish using plain savoury pancakes
instead of pasta.

For 8–10 main course helpings, use:

For the spinach filling
25 g (1 oz) butter
2 x 15 ml spoons (2 tablespoons) olive oil
275 g (10 oz) onion, sliced
2 cloves garlic, crushed
675 g (1½ lb) frozen spinach (defrosted)*
2 eggs
50 ml (2 fl oz) single cream
25 g (1 oz) flour
salt and pepper
grated nutmeg to taste (I use ⅛ of a whole nutmeg)
grated rind of 1 lemon
25 g (1 oz) grated Parmesan, *or* 50 g (2 oz) Emmenthal or
   Cheddar cheese
325–350 g (12 oz) cottage cheese

For the béchamel sauce
50 g (2 oz) butter
50 g (2 oz) flour
700 ml (1¼ pints) milk
1 x 5 ml spoon (1 teaspoon) mustard powder
grated nutmeg
salt and pepper
100–125 g (4 oz) Cheddar cheese, grated

---

*If you have a food processor, use leaf or chopped spinach. If not, use creamed or
chopped spinach.

Additional ingredients

16–20 cannelloni tubes (approx.)
150 ml (¼ pint) single cream
50 g (2 oz) Cheddar cheese
225 g (8 oz) chopped watercress (optional)

Stew the onions and the garlic in the butter and oil in a covered pan over a low heat for 20 minutes, removing the lid and stirring vigorously every few minutes.

If the spinach is chopped or whole leaf, force out any excess water through a sieve. Remove the onion from the heat, and mix in the spinach. At this point, if you have a food processor and are using whole leaf or chopped spinach, put the onion and spinach mixture into the processor for a couple of minutes until it is finely chopped but not creamed. (You may need to do this in batches.)

Beat the eggs, cream, flour, salt, pepper, nutmeg and lemon rind together in a bowl. Combine this mixture and the Parmesan and cottage cheese with the spinach and onion mixture.

Make the béchamel sauce with the ingredients stated, following the instructions on page 224. Add the 100–125 g (4 oz) grated cheese at the last minute.

Precook the cannelloni for a few minutes in salted, boiling water (see page 6). I know manufacturers recommend using it uncooked, but in my experience there is a real danger the pasta will not absorb enough liquid and will arrive at the table still glutinous.

Stuff the cannelloni with the spinach mixture, and lay the pieces in an ovenproof dish, spreading any remaining filling on top. Add the chopped watercress to the béchamel sauce and pour over the whole dish. Pour over the single cream and sprinkle with the extra Cheddar. Cover tightly with foil and cook in a medium oven (190°C/375°F/gas mark 5) for about an hour, removing the foil after the first 45 minutes. If the dish is not sufficiently browned on top, place under a hot grill for another few minutes before serving.

42 Baked tagliatelle with spinach, eggs and cheese

A very pleasant and economical supper or lunch dish – a lot easier than lasagne but with the added advantage of being baked, so it can be prepared in advance. If you can't find fresh spinach in the shops and don't want to use frozen, you could always substitute spring greens, sliced and then steamed or boiled.

As I keep saying, I'm not such a fan of the shop-bought fresh (or pasteurised) tagliatelle. I recommend using a good-quality dried tagliatelle. Along with most of the inhabitants of Rome, I use for all my pasta cooking the Italian make of F. lli de Cecco di Filippo, instantly recognisable by its turquoise and yellow packets, and in this case I would use their pasta all'uovo. If this is not available I use another excellent make, Barilla.

For 4–6 main course helpings, use:

25 g (1 oz) butter
100–125 g (4 oz) onion, finely sliced
1–2 cloves garlic, crushed
450 g (1 lb) fresh spinach, or 225 g (8 oz) frozen spinach, chopped or leaf
rind of ½ lemon, grated
grated nutmeg to taste
125 ml (4 fl oz) cream
6 eggs
225 g (8 oz) tagliatelle

For the béchamel sauce
25–50 g (1½ oz) butter
25–50 g (1½ oz) flour
575 ml (1 pint) milk
100–125 g (4 oz) Cheddar cheese, grated, or substitute ½ quantity Emmenthal or fresh Parmesan

Sauté the onion and garlic in the butter until softened and translucent. Carefully wash the spinach in lots of cold water. In a medium to large pan steam the spinach (covered) in a few tablespoons (15 ml spoons) water and milk. It will reduce its bulk quite considerably, so if at first all the spinach does not fit in the pan, don't worry, just keep adding more as it shrinks. If using frozen, cook according to instructions on the packet. Strain, pressing the spinach against the colander or sieve to remove as much liquid as possible. Chop the spinach coarsely (if not already chopped), then add to the onion and garlic in the pan. Sauté for a further few minutes before adding the lemon rind and nutmeg (a few gratings, to taste) and then the cream and seasoning.

Boil the eggs for about 7–8 minutes (or 10 if they are straight from the fridge). Cool them in cold water, and then remove the shells.

Make the béchamel sauce, following the instructions on page 224. Stir in half the grated cheese.

Cook the tagliatelle in plenty of salted, boiling water until 'al dente'. Drain, and put back into the pan with a spoonful of oil or butter. Toss together and leave while you prepare for the next stage. (If you have, as recommended, used good-quality dried pasta and cooked it until 'al dente' it will sit quite happily for as long as you like without sticking together!)

Using an ovenproof dish about the size of a large soufflé dish, spread the spinach mixture over the bottom and then lay the eggs (whole) on top at regular intervals. Spread the tagliatelle evenly over the eggs and spinach, pour over the béchamel sauce, and sprinkle over the remaining cheese. Cover the dish with foil and bake in a preheated oven (190°C/375°F/gas mark 5) for 30 minutes (at least), removing the foil for the last 15 minutes to allow the dish to brown. If it still does not seem brown enough, place under a hot grill for a few minutes, and then serve immediately.

43 Aubergine, tomato and cheese lasagne

I have to admit that I find lasagne hard work! I am not a perfectly organised cook in a perfect kitchen, nor am I particularly patient, and indeed on one occasion ended up with pots and pans everywhere, tomato sauce on the floor and walls (something to do with detaching the food processor too quickly) and burnt fingers from trying to handle the lasagne before I had rinsed it.

The big advantage of lasagne (and all baked pastas) is that everything can be prepared beforehand, so that if you are making a dinner for friends, by the time they arrive the kitchen can be spotless and the dish itself happily bubbling away in the oven – a big advantage when entertaining on your own.

This dish I originally created for my parents, uncle and aunt. Auntie Christine is a strict vegetarian, whilst my father basically believed a meal wasn't a meal if it didn't include meat or fish. This lasagne fitted the bill perfectly – although meatless, it is substantial and special enough for any occasion, and spectacular, with its contrasting blacks, yellows and reds.

Serve with a luscious mixed green salad, if possible throwing in watercress or rocket (arugula), avocado, mushrooms, walnuts and anything else out of the ordinary. If you can't face juggling with the lasagne leaves, then make the dish substituting tagliatelle layered in with the other ingredients in the same manner.

For 6 main course helpings, use:

675 g (1½ lb) aubergine (egg plant)
olive oil
a little flour
4 eggs, hard-boiled
2 Italian Mozzarella cheeses (300 g/10 oz) *or* substitute
175 g (6 oz) Gruyère, Emmenthal *or* mild Cheddar, *or* a combination, in each case thinly sliced
75–100 g (3 oz) freshly grated Gruyère *or* Emmenthal,

or substitute Cheddar, *and*: 25–50 g (1½ oz) freshly
   grated Parmesan, or extra of one of the above cheeses
275–325 g (10–12 oz) lasagne, or wholewheat lasagne
sea salt and freshly ground black pepper

For the tomato sauce
2 x 15 ml spoons (2 tablespoons) olive oil
100–125 g (4 oz) onion, finely sliced
1 dried red chilli (about 3 cm/1¼ inches long), finely
   chopped but including seeds
4 cloves garlic, crushed
800 g (1 lb 12 oz) tinned Italian plum tomatoes
3 x 15 ml spoons (3 tablespoons) tomato purée
2 x 5 ml (2 teaspoons) sugar
2 or 3 bay leaves
2 x 5 ml spoons (2 teaspoons) dried oregano

For the béchamel sauce
25 g (1 oz) butter
25 g (1 oz) flour
1 x 5 ml spoon (1 teaspoon) English mustard powder
575 ml (1 pint) milk
25 g (1 oz) onion
few peppercorns
2 or 3 bay leaves

Cut the aubergines into slices about 0.5 cm (¼ inch) thick.
Lay the slices on some kitchen roll or a clean tea towel,
sprinkle lightly with salt, and leave to sweat. After about 15
minutes turn them over, and leave to sweat for another 15
minutes. Lightly flour the pieces on both sides, and fry in
olive oil. Alternatively, arrange on generously oiled baking
sheets, dribble a little more oil on top of the slices and bake
for about half an hour in a hot oven (200°C/400°F /gas mark
6), turning them over every 7 minutes or so and adding more
oil if necessary. (Aubergines do tend to absorb a lot of oil
which is not so good for the waistline or the bank balance
but, all the same, very good for the taste.) When cooked, put
the aubergines aside until ready to layer into the lasagne.

Mash the hard-boiled eggs with a fork. Make a basic tomato sauce, following the instructions in recipe 59, on page 125, using two of the garlic cloves, crushed, at the beginning of the cooking and throwing in the other two, crushed, just before taking the sauce off the heat. Make a thin béchamel sauce following instructions on page 224, using version (1). Cook the lasagne as instructed on page 6.

Take a shallow, ovenproof dish, no more than 8–10 cm (3 or 4 inches) deep and about 38 cm (15 inches) by 25.5 cm (10 inches). I use an attractive oval earthenware dish which I can bring to the table. Spread a thin layer of the tomato sauce across the bottom, followed by a sprinkling of the egg, and a couple of tablespoons of the béchamel, then a sprinkling of the grated cheeses. Now spread a double layer of the lasagne (or tagliatelle). Then start again with the filling ingredients, this time including a layer of the aubergine and the thinly sliced Mozzarella (these two ingredients are fairly rich, so the layer should not be too dense), and seasoning with a sprinkling of sea salt and black pepper. Follow by a double layer of lasagne. Carry on with these layers as long as the ingredients last, ending with tomato sauce, béchamel, and a good sprinkling of the grated cheese.

Cover with foil so that the pasta will absorb some of the juices, and bake in a hot oven (200°C/400°F/gas mark 6) for about an hour, removing the foil for the last 10 or 15 minutes to allow the top to brown.

44 Bows with spinach, mascarpone (or cream cheese) and roast red peppers

A simple, easy to cook dish and very pretty with the green of the spinach, red of pepper and cream of the pasta with mascarpone.

If you like spicy tastes, then use more chilli and garlic at the tossing the pasta stage, or even run up a little spicy tomato sauce (see instructions in recipe 40 on page 90) and add.

If you have no spinach, you could easily use another vegetable, such as sliced courgettes, broccoli florets, French beans or even peas.

For 3 starter size or 2 main course helpings, use:

2 x 15 ml spoons (2 tablespoons) butter
225 g (8 oz) leaf spinach (frozen or fresh), coarsely chopped
2 cloves garlic, crushed
grated lemon rind
nutmeg (optional)
2 small or 1 large red pepper *or* substitute 50 g (2 oz) sun-dried tomatoes, coarsely chopped
1 x 15 ml spoon (1 tablespoon) olive oil
1 small dried chilli (optional)
225 g (8 oz) bows or shells
4 x 15 ml spoons (4 tablespoons) mascarpone cheese *or* substitute cream or cottage cheese
25 g (1 oz) toasted pine kernels or broken walnuts (optional)
10 basil leaves (optional)
fresh Parmesan

Cook the spinach on a low heat in a covered pan with 1 x 15 ml spoon (1 tablespoon) butter, 1 of the cloves of crushed garlic, and a *little* grated lemon rind and nutmeg (if using). Stir frequently and watch carefully. It shouldn't need any

more liquid, but if it does, add 1–2 x 15 ml spoons
(1–2 tablespoons) water.

Place the whole red pepper on the grill pan, with the
pepper nearly touching the heating element, and grill under a
high heat. (Most of the skin will turn black but will peel off
to reveal an unburnt, delicious pepper underneath.) Remove
from the grill, cool slightly and peel, then cut the peeled
pepper into strips and lay on a plate. Chop coarsely and
dribble 1 x 15 ml spoon (1 tablespoon) of the olive oil over
the chopped pepper and leave aside.

Sauté the remaining clove of garlic and the chilli in the
remaining spoon of oil for less than a minute, being *very* careful not to let the garlic burn. Toast the pine kernels, if using.
See instructions in recipe 38 on page 85.

Meanwhile, cook the pasta in plenty of salted, boiling
water until it is 'al dente'. Drain and put back into the pan
with the oil, sautéed garlic and chilli. Toss with the mascarpone or cream cheese until the pasta is evenly coated. Add the
spinach, red peppers, half the pine kernels or nuts and grated
nutmeg (if using) and toss again over a low heat until the
ingredients are well heated through.

Serve immediately with the remaining pine kernels and the
basil leaves sprinkled on top, and with freshly grated
Parmesan cheese on the side.

45 Quills with celery, stilton, mascarpone (or cream), vodka, fresh herbs and optional pistachios

People seem to love the idea (and the taste) of these pasta dishes incorporating vodka! This dish is quite rich, very tasty, and pretty to look at, so I would recommend serving it as a starter.

You could prepare the sauce in advance, heat it through and toss it with the pasta at the last minute.

For 3–4 starter size or 2 main course helpings, use:

1½ x 15 ml spoons (1½ tablespoons) butter
3 spring onions, finely chopped (if not using herbs)
175 g (6 oz) celery, finely sliced (green, if possible)
175 g (6 oz) Stilton (or other soft or hard blue cheese), coarsely chopped or crumbled
6 x 15 ml spoons (6 tablespoons) mascarpone cheese or cream (or a combination)
5 x 15 ml spoons (5 tablespoons) vodka
225–275 g (8–10 oz) small quills or shells
1 x 15 ml spoon (1 tablespoon) mint or chives, finely chopped, *or* 1 x 5 ml spoon (1 teaspoon) thyme
25 g (1 oz) pistachio nuts, shelled and chopped into quarters (optional)

Sauté the onions (if using) and celery in the butter over a low heat until softened and beginning to turn golden.

Add the blue cheese and then the mascarpone (or cream). Stir together until the cheese has melted and then add the vodka. If you wish to reduce the alcohol content, then turn up the heat and let the mixture bubble gently for about 30 seconds.

Meanwhile, cook the pasta in plenty of salted, boiling water until 'al dente'. Drain and put back into the pot. Toss the pasta in the sauce on a low heat until heated through and then serve with herbs (and nuts, if using) sprinkled on top, and freshly grated Parmesan on the side.

46 Cold pasta salad with chickpeas, boiled eggs, cherry tomatoes, walnuts, herbs and capers

Cold pasta salads are usually too insipid for my taste. By tossing the tomatoes or chickpeas in the garlic and chilli, and adding balsamic vinegar and capers, I think I have brought this salad somewhat to life. There are other ingredients which could be added to bring a further 'kick', such as fresh arugula (rocket) leaves torn into pieces; 50 g (a couple of ounces) of coarsely chopped sun-dried tomatoes; or, if you eat fish, a few coarsely chopped anchovies.

For a variation, try substituting lightly fried courgette slices for the tomatoes, or adding a tin of flaked tuna (drained of its oil or brine).

For 3 main course or 3–4 salad size helpings, use:

2 eggs
1 x 15 ml (1 tablespoon) olive oil
1 dried chilli (to taste)
1 clove garlic, crushed
8–10 cherry tomatoes, halved
250 g chickpeas (cooked, tinned)
   or substitute tinned butter beans
1 x 15 ml (1 heaped tablespoon) mint and/or parsley, or
   coriander, chopped
25 g (1 oz) walnuts, coarsely chopped
2 x 15 ml spoons (2 tablespoons) capers, drained and then
   chopped
fresh Parmesan, coarsely grated (optional)
275–325 g (10–12 oz) pasta twists or shells

For the salad dressing
1½ x 15 ml spoons (1½ tablespoons) balsamic vinegar
4½ x 15 ml spoons (4½ tablespoons) olive oil

1 x 5 ml spoon (1 teaspoon) mustard (English,
    Dijon or grained)
sea salt and black pepper
1 x 5 ml spoon (1 teaspoon) caster sugar

Hard-boil the eggs (in boiling water for 6 or 7 minutes), rinse
in cold water, remove the shell and coarsely chop.

Sauté the chilli and garlic in the olive oil for a few seconds,
throw in the tomatoes and give them a quick sizzle. Add the
chickpeas and herbs, toss for a few seconds. Remove from the
heat and allow to cool. Put the salad dressing ingredients into
a small bowl or cup and beat together with a fork. Put aside.

Meanwhile, cook the pasta in plenty of salted, boiling
water until 'al dente'. Drain and put in the serving bowl. Toss
with the tomato, chickpeas and herbs, the walnuts, capers
and the salad dressing. Add the grated cheese (if using) and
serve with extra herbs sprinkled on top.

47 Twists with pesto, mascarpone cheese (or crème fraîche) and ricotta

Another quick and easy winner. I'm amazed by how many supermarkets now stock ricotta, in little tubs, but if you don't have any then leave it out and use a little extra Parmesan cheese and maybe even some diced Mozzarella. I really wouldn't recommend using cottage cheese.

For 3–4 starter size or 2 main course helpings, use:

2 x 15 ml spoons (2 tablespoons) olive oil
1 clove garlic, crushed
1 small dried chilli, finely chopped
2 x 15 ml spoons (2 tablespoons) pesto (chilled or bottled)
3 x 15 ml spoons (3 tablespoons) mascarpone cheese, or crème fraîche (or substitute cream)
125 g (4 oz) ricotta
225–275 g (8–10 oz) twists
8–10 basil leaves (when available)
freshly grated Parmesan

Sauté the garlic and the chilli in one of the spoons of olive oil for just a few seconds. Stir in the pesto sauce, and then the mascarpone (crème fraîche or cream) and half the ricotta.

Meanwhile, cook the pasta in plenty of salted, boiling water until 'al dente'. Drain, put back into the pan, toss with the remaining spoonful of oil, spoon onto the sauce and toss again over a low flame until heated through.

Serve immediately with the remaining ricotta and the basil leaves sprinkled on top and Parmesan cheese served on the side.

48 Spaghetti with simple traditional tomato sauce

One of the most delicious pasta dishes I have ever eaten was pasta served with a simple tomato sauce. I was on the Greek island of Patmos, and I suppose it was the quality of the ingredients – fresh plum tomatoes, local olive oil and freshly picked herbs from the mountainside – which made such a simple sauce so exquisite. Stories about my summer holidays are of course of little consolation to the English cook struggling with locally available ingredients. Nevertheless, an English version of the classic Italian tomato sauce is also delicious when carefully prepared and gently stewed for an adequate length of time.

The good news is that the quality of tomatoes available in the British shops has improved no end in the past few years. However, the *really* good tomatoes (vine tomatoes, cherry and so on) are still very expensive and so I would recommend using *tinned* unless you have an abundance in your own garden.

For 2 main course helpings, use:

3 x 15 ml spoons (3 tablespoons) olive oil
100–125 g (4 oz) onion, chopped
2 cloves garlic, crushed
1 small dried chilli (for taste), crumbled (optional)
450 g (1 lb) fresh tomatoes, skinned and coarsely chopped,
    or 400 g (14 oz) tinned Italian plum tomatoes
1 x 5 ml spoon (1 teaspoon) sugar (optional)
herbs to taste (e.g. 2 x 5 ml spoons/2 teaspoons dried
    oregano) *or* fresh chopped tarragon or thyme or
    torn basil
salt and pepper
225–275 g (8–10 oz) spaghetti
freshly grated Parmesan cheese

Sauté the onion and garlic in the oil over a low heat for several minutes until the onion is translucent. Add the chilli (if using), tomatoes, sugar, herbs and seasoning. (If you are using tinned tomatoes break them up in the pan with a wooden spoon.) Simmer in a covered pan for 20–25 minutes, stirring frequently.

Meanwhile, cook the pasta in plenty of salted, boiling water until 'al dente'. Drain, and put back into the pan or into a preheated serving dish. Add the sauce and mix together well.

Serve with grated cheese on the side.

49 Tagliatelle (or frills) in a carrot, parsnip and cumin soup with courgettes, asparagus (or cabbage or broccoli) and coriander

This is one of those marvellous dishes which is practically a meal in itself. It's also scrumptious and exceptionally pretty to look at, especially if you can find one *yellow* and one *green* courgette. The 'soup' is not so much a soup as a generous sauce. Adjust the cumin and chilli flavourings according to *your* taste. Remember, it's easier to add more later than to take away.

I used my favourite Marks and Spencer egg pasta, 'Fiorelli' (little flowers, I assume), though I like to think of them as 'frills', which I think substitutes well for tagliatelle and is easier to handle. You could make a variation, leaving out the Parmesan cheese and including 225 g (8 oz) firm bean curd or tofu cut into cubes and 50 g (2 oz) toasted sesame seeds, both added at the end. This dish is good enough to serve at dinner to guests, but be especially careful not to overspice it.

For 4 main course helpings, use:

- 4 x 15 ml spoons (4 tablespoons) olive or vegetable oil or butter
- 100 g (4 oz) onion, sliced or chopped
- 2 cloves garlic, crushed
- 225 g (8 oz) parsnip, sliced or chopped
- 225 g (8 oz) carrot, sliced or chopped
- 500 ml (1 pint) water or vegetable stock
- a couple of pinches cumin seeds or ground cumin powder (or substitute curry powder)
- 1 small packet asparagus tips (100 g/4 oz) *or* substitute 100 g (4 oz) broccoli spears or cabbage, finely sliced
- 1 or 2 courgettes (about 175–225 g/6–8 oz), halved and then sliced

½ small dried or fresh chilli (to taste), finely chopped

1 medium leek (about 225 g/8 oz), carefully washed and
  finely sliced

225–275 g (8–10 oz) tagliatelle or fiorelli

fresh coriander leaves, chopped (if available, or substitute
  parsley, basil or chives)

freshly grated Parmesan (or see variation in introduction)

Sauté the onion and one of the crushed cloves of garlic in a medium-sized saucepan in 1 x 15 ml spoon (1 tablespoon) of the oil or butter until softened. Add the parsnip and carrot and sauté for another minute or so. Pour over the water or stock and simmer on a low heat for about 15 minutes or until the vegetables soften. Purée in the liquidiser or food processor. Stir in the ground cumin, to taste.

Steam or parboil the asparagus (or broccoli spears or cabbage) and courgettes until just soft.

Sauté the chilli, the remaining clove of garlic and the sliced leek in the remaining 3 x 15 ml spoons (3 tablespoons) oil or butter until softened. Pour over the parsnip and carrot soup, add the steamed or parboiled vegetables, adding more cumin seed or cumin powder if necessary.

Meanwhile, cook the pasta in plenty of salted, boiling water until 'al dente'. Drain, pour over the sauce and mix together carefully, using a wooden spoon.

Serve immediately with the chopped herbs spread on top, and freshly grated Parmesan on the side.

50 Aubergine, porcini, leek or pea mould ('sformata')

Follow recipe 40 on page 90 for the mould with aubergine, tomato and cheese, only instead of the béchamel, tomato and pesto sauces, make either:

(1) the tagliatelle with leeks and porcini, recipe 53, page 115 (double quantity of sauce);
(2) the tagliatelle with dried and fresh mushrooms, recipe 39, page 88 (one and a half times the quantity of sauce); or
(3) the tagliatelle with dried porcini (or cep) mushrooms, crème fraîche and walnuts, recipe 56, page 119 (double quantity of sauce).

If using 2 or 3 then you can add 225 g (8 oz) peas – frozen, fresh or tinned – cooked, stirring them in at the end just before putting into the mould.

Make double the quantity of sauce only – not the pasta. Use about 250 g (8–10 oz) tagliatelle.

51 Spaghetti with puréed roast red pepper, chilli and tomato

This recipe was given to me by a very good friend, Rosamond Freeman-Attwood, who leads an extremely hectic life as an actress, author, wife and mother, and writing scripts and plays, sometimes with me. She adapted the ingredients from a Tunisian recipe. Ros and her husband give dinner parties at least twice a week to hordes of marauding fellow actors and other friends. She is an enthusiast of my first two books, *Pastability* and *Pastability: A Second Helping*, and swears by pasta because it is quick and easy to prepare and always enormously popular.

For 4 main course or 6 starter size helpings, use:

   3 red peppers (approx. 450 g/1 lb)
   3 x 15 ml spoons (3 tablespoons) olive oil
   325–350 g (12 oz) tomatoes, peeled and coarsely chopped
   2–4 cloves garlic, crushed
   ½ x 5 ml spoon (½ teaspoon) chilli powder (to taste)
   salt and ground black pepper
   100–175 g (4–6 oz) green beans or mange-tout (snow
      peas) (optional)
   325–350 g (12 oz) spaghetti, or quills
   12–15 black olives, pitted and coarsely chopped
   2 hard-boiled eggs, finely chopped, or mashed with a fork

Place the whole peppers on the grill pan, with the flesh almost touching the heating element, and grill on a high heat on all sides until the peppers turn completely black. Allow to cool and then peel off the black, burnt skin.* Cut into halves, remove the stalk and seeds and then slice the softened pepper

---

*It is a well-known tip to put the hot, scorched red peppers into a covered dish or plastic bag and leave until cool. This will make the skin easier to peel off. However, the last time I tried this method, I made the mistake of *picking up* the plastic bag (with the hot peppers inside) to move it. The peppers fell straight through the bag, onto the floor!

into strips and lay out on a plate. Dribble a spoonful or so of the oil over the strips, and leave for 10 minutes or while you prepare the rest of the ingredients.

Skin the tomatoes by putting them in a pan of lightly boiling water for just a minute or so (the water in which you are about to boil the pasta will do just fine!). Scoop them out with a slotted spoon, peel them and chop coarsely. Put the peppers, tomatoes, garlic, chilli powder, and some salt and freshly ground black pepper in a liquidiser or food processor and blend. You should find that you have a sauce with the consistency and colour of tinned tomato soup.

Steam or lightly boil the green beans or mange-tout (if using) for a couple of minutes until just cooked but still crunchy and green. Cut into 2.5 cm (1 inch) pieces.

Meanwhile, cook the pasta in plenty of salted, boiling water until 'al dente', drain, and return to the pan with the sauce.

Toss the sauce and pasta in the pan until well heated through then add the beans (if using). At the last moment before serving, sprinkle over the olives and egg.

52 Quills with spicy tomatoes and aubergine

The long list of ingredients makes this recipe look more complicated than it is. It's a good vegetarian dish for those who like their vegetables slightly exotic and spicy.

For 2 main course or 3–4 starter size helpings, use:

  1 large or 2 small aubergines (275–325 g/10–12 oz)
  2 x 15 ml (2 tablespoons) vegetable or nut oil
  75–100 g (3 oz) onion, finely chopped
  2 cloves garlic, crushed
  2 x 5 ml spoons (2 teaspoons) fresh root ginger, finely grated
  ½ x 5 ml spoon (½ teaspoon) ground coriander
  ¼ x 5 ml spoon (¼ teaspoon) chilli powder
  275 g (10 oz) tinned Italian plum tomatoes, chopped
  2 x 15 ml spoons (2 tablespoons) white wine or stock
  2 x 5 ml spoons (2 teaspoons) tomato purée
  4 x 15 ml spoons (4 tablespoons) low-fat yoghurt
  200 g (7 oz) quills or shells
  2 x 15 ml spoons (2 tablespoons) fresh coriander, finely chopped (optional)

Wrap the aubergines in foil and cook in a medium to hot oven (200°C/400°F/gas mark 6) for 40 minutes. Cut them in half, scoop out the flesh and mash. Slice the skin into thin strips.

Sauté the onion in the oil until softened and translucent. Add the garlic, ginger, ground coriander and chilli powder and continue to sauté for a couple of minutes. Add the aubergine pulp and continue to cook over a medium flame for another 3 or 4 minutes. Add the chopped tomatoes, wine and tomato purée and simmer for another 7 or 8 minutes, stirring occasionally. At the last moment before adding to the pasta, carefully stir in the yoghurt.

Meanwhile, cook the pasta in plenty of salted, boiling water until 'al dente', drain, and put back into the pan. Pour over the sauce and heat through carefully. At the last moment add the aubergine skins and the fresh coriander (if using). Serve immediately on preheated plates.

53 Tagliatelle with leeks and porcini mushrooms

A really delicious and rather exotic combination – the rich taste of the porcini blends particularly well with the cream and the egg pasta. Serve as a starter on any occasion, but be prepared for requests for second and third helpings!

For 2–3 main course or 4 starter size helpings, use:

15 g (½ oz) dried porcini mushrooms
2 x 15 ml spoons (2 tablespoons) butter
175 g (6 oz) leeks, sliced
4 x 15 ml spoons (4 tablespoons) double or single cream
1 x 15 ml spoon (1 tablespoon) white wine, or dry Martini
sea salt and freshly ground black pepper
175 g (6 oz) tagliatelle

Put the porcini into a small bowl and cover with a wine glass full of water. Leave to soak for 20 minutes. Sauté the sliced leeks in the butter until softened, cover, and stew in their own juices for the next 10 minutes over a low flame, stirring every so often and taking care not to let them burn.

Drain the mushrooms, reserving the liquid. Chop the mushrooms into smallish pieces, and then add them and their soaking liquid to the leeks and butter. Continue cooking for a few minutes until the liquid has reduced by about half. Stir in the cream and white wine and add seasoning. Heat through gently just before adding to the pasta.

Meanwhile, cook the pasta in plenty of salted, boiling water until 'al dente', drain and put into a preheated serving dish. Pour on the reheated sauce and mix together thoroughly. Serve immediately, and avoid cheese unless people demand it – this dish is better without.

54 Rigatoni with onions, cheese and olives

A very satisfying and tasty dish, this also has the advantage of being a 'store cupboard standby', as most people have an onion or two kicking around somewhere in their food cupboard and some sort of cheese in the fridge.

For 2 main course helpings, use:

1 x 15 ml spoon (1 tablespoon) olive oil
1 x 15 ml spoon (1 tablespoon) butter
175 g (6 oz) white onions
175 g (6 oz) red onions (or substitute more white onions)
½ a pepper – red, yellow or green – *or* substitute
   courgette or carrot or even frozen peas
1 small dried chilli, chopped, to taste
3 cloves garlic, coarsely chopped
8 olives
1 x 15 ml spoon (1 tablespoon) capers, drained and chopped
2 x 5 ml spoons (2 teaspoons) dried or fresh herbs
   (e.g. oregano or thyme)
225 g (8 oz) rigatoni
about 50 g (2 oz) freshly grated Parmesan, Cheddar,
   Cheshire or Gruyère; or substitute any other cheese you
   happen to have.

Sauté the onions, pepper, chilli and garlic in the oil and butter for a couple of minutes in a small pan with a lid. Then put on the lid and stew on a very low heat for about 20 minutes, stirring occasionally. Throw in the olives, chopped capers and herbs.

Meanwhile, cook the pasta in plenty of salted, boiling water until 'al dente'. Then drain the pasta and return it to the pan. Add the sauce and toss together over a low flame until the pasta is nice and hot and well integrated with the sauce. Add the grated cheese, and toss again. Serve immediately, with additional grated cheese on the side.

55 Shells with spicy Indian aubergine, tomato, red pepper and chickpeas

This is another dish influenced by vegetarian Indian cuisine.

For 2 main course helpings, use:

1 aubergine (approx. 225 g/8 oz)
100–125 g (4 oz) onion, coarsely chopped
1 x 15 ml spoon (1 tablespoon) ginger, peeled and coarsely chopped
3 cloves garlic
1–2 dried red chillies (to taste)
2 x 15 ml spoons (2 tablespoons) oil
¼ x 5 ml spoon (¼ teaspoon) mustard seeds
¼ x 5 ml spoon (¼ teaspoon) cumin seeds
½ x 5 ml spoon (½ teaspoon) ground coriander
¼ x 5 ml spoon (¼ teaspoon) garam marsala
125 g (4 oz) tinned tomatoes
1 x 5 ml spoon (1 teaspoon) tomato purée
1½ x 5 ml spoons (1½ teaspoons) sugar
210 ml (7½ fl oz) water
½ red pepper, chopped
125 g (4 oz) tinned chickpeas
2 x 15 ml spoons (2 heaped tablespoons) yoghurt
275 g (10 oz) shells
chopped coriander leaves (or mint or parsley)

Slice the aubergine, sprinkle with salt and leave to drain on some kitchen paper for 20 minutes or so. Then cut each 'disc' into 4 or 8 pieces.

Chop very finely (or purée in a small food processor or blender) the onion with the ginger, garlic and chilli.

Sauté the mustard seeds in the oil until they start to pop. Add the cumin, ground coriander and garam marsala, and stir-fry for another minute or so. Add the puréed or finely chopped onion, ginger, garlic and chilli and continue to stir-fry for another minute. Add the tinned tomatoes, the tomato purée, the sugar, the water, the red pepper and the aubergines, stir together and then simmer over a low heat for 20 minutes or until the aubergine pieces are cooked. Add the chickpeas and the yoghurt. Stir together and cook on a low heat for a further 5 minutes.

Meanwhile, cook the pasta in plenty of salted, boiling water until 'al dente'. Then drain it and return it to the pan.

Toss the pasta with the sauce and serve with the chopped herbs sprinkled on top.

56 Home-made tagliatelle with dried porcini (or cep) mushrooms, crème fraîche (or cream) and walnuts

This is a comparatively simple sauce to prepare, quite rich, and complements well the flavours of fresh tagliatelle.

You can make your own fresh tagliatelle if you have the equipment and/or the elbow power (see recipe 105, page 222). Or you can buy fresh tagliatelle in the chilled section of most good supermarkets. Failing this, F. lli de Cecco and Barilla make excellent dried egg tagliatelle; in fact, it is just as tasty as home-made, and less work.

For 2 main course helpings, use:

25 g (1 oz) dried porcini (or cep) mushrooms
2 shallots (or 1 small onion, 75 g/3 oz), finely sliced
25 g (1 oz) butter
6 x 15 ml spoons (6 tablespoons) crème fraîche,
    double or single cream
225–275 g (8–10 oz) fresh tagliatelle
25 g (1 oz) walnuts, coarsely chopped
fresh Parmesan
freshly ground black pepper

Soak the dried mushrooms in a small cupful of warm water for about 20 minutes. Drain, reserving the liquid, and chop coarsely.

Sauté the shallots or onion in the butter for a minute or two until the onion softens, add the porcini (or cep) mushrooms and sauté for another 30 seconds. Now add the crème fraîche or cream and the reserved liquid from the mushrooms. Stir on a low heat for a minute or two.

Meanwhile, cook the tagliatelle in plenty of salted, boiling water until 'al dente', drain and return to the pan. Pour over the sauce and toss with the pasta until well heated through. Serve immediately with the chopped walnuts sprinkled on top, and freshly grated Parmesan cheese and black pepper on the side.

57 Shop-bought fresh stuffed ravioli with roast vegetables, Mozzarella and herbs

The Italian and pasta-related ingredients available in good supermarkets have improved beyond measure over the past ten years. You can now find ricotta, fresh Parmesan and Mozzarella, vine tomatoes and pesto sauce even in the smaller branches of, say, Sainsbury's or Tesco, buried in the outskirts of a small country town, and my local Waitrose in the Finchley Road, north London, is a positive Mecca.

My one great disappointment in all the supermarkets, and even the Italian delicatessens, is the stuffed pastas. The packets bear extravagant promises of asparagus tips, artichoke hearts, garlic, herbs and three cheeses; or spinach with ricotta, garlic, Parmesan and basil. In my experience, the fillings turn out to be some sort of grey gunge, looking and tasting like wet sawdust. Then, when I cook the stuff, if I leave the stove for a minute and the pasta water boils a little too fast, or I inadvertently stir it, then these stuffed pastas instantly fall to pieces, filling the whole saucepan with an unsavoury-looking grey mess.

However, *you* may have found a filled pasta which is an exception, or you may even enjoy the taste of soft sawdust. If you do find yourself cooking a shop-bought stuffed pasta, then the following is a good way of enlivening it and making it go further. In this way you can turn a small pack into a complete meal for two or three people.

Instead of using the pesto sauce described, you could make the simple tomato sauce (recipe 48 on page 106) or the blue cheese sauce (recipe 45 on page 102), with or without the vodka, or even just add some chopped herbs, sea salt and crushed garlic to some extra melted butter or olive oil.

For 2–3 main course helpings, use:

about 3–4 x 15 ml spoons (3–4 tablespoons) olive oil
2 cloves garlic, crushed
1 small dried chilli, crumbled (optional, to taste)
fresh herbs (2–3 x 15 ml spoons/2–3 tablespoons) of whatever herbs you have available.
50–125 g (2–4 oz) Mozzarella, cut into medium-size cubes,
  a little smaller than the vegetable pieces
1 packet (250 g/8.8 oz) ravioli or tortellini or any stuffed
  fresh pasta

Any selection (3 or 4) of the following
4 medium tomatoes, cut in half
4 small onions, parboiled
2 small courgettes, cut into quarters, parboiled
1 small sweet potato or yam, baked in the oven for an hour
  and then cut into thick slices
2 medium parsnips, cut into quarters crosswise, and then
  halves lengthwise, and then roasted in the oven
6 small to medium Brussels sprouts, parboiled

For the pesto sauce
1 clove garlic, crushed
2 x 15 ml spoons (2 tablespoons) olive oil
2 x 15 ml spoons (2 tablespoons) pesto sauce,
  bottled or chilled
2 x 15 ml spoons (2 tablespoons) cream or crème fraîche
  (optional)
freshly grated Parmesan

Sauté the garlic and chilli in the olive oil for half a minute or
so. Then add your selection of vegetables, and your fresh
chopped herbs and sauté for 10 or 15 minutes, turning gently
with a wooden spoon until most of the vegetable surfaces
have turned golden. Add the Mozzarella cheese, season to
taste and continue to sauté for a couple of minutes.

To make the sauce, sauté the garlic quickly in the oil. Stir in
the pesto sauce (and cream or crème fraîche, if using). Heat

through gently just before serving.

Meanwhile, cook the pasta, following the directions on the packet. Drain and put back in the pan with just a little oil or butter to keep it moist.

Place a portion of the roasted vegetables, herb and Mozzarella mixture on each plate and serve the ravioli on top. Pour over the sauce and then serve with freshly grated Parmesan on the side.

58 Wholewheat shells with fennel, cherry tomatoes, tofu and toasted sesame seeds

A handy basic recipe combining fennel and chickpeas with tofu and sesame seeds. Feel free to substitute other ingredients for the tomatoes (if you can't find any really *tasty* tomatoes), such as broccoli, peppers or courgettes, adding them at the same time as the fennel so that they get the extra cooking time.

For 2–3 main course helpings, use:

  2 x 15 ml spoons (2 tablespoons) sesame seeds
  100–125 g (4 oz) tofu
  1 x 15 ml spoon (1 tablespoon) vegetable oil
    or sesame seed oil
  2 x 15 ml spoons (2 tablespoons) olive oil
  1 small or medium chilli (optional), chopped or crumbled
  2 cloves garlic, crushed
  75 g (3 oz) onion, finely sliced
  100–125 g (4 oz) fennel, finely sliced
  2 x 15 ml spoons (2 tablespoons) white wine, or apple
    juice, or water
  100–125 g (4 oz) cherry tomatoes (or vine or tasty
    'home-grown'), halved or quartered
  100–125 g (4 oz) chickpeas
  wholewheat shells
  8 olives
  coriander, *or* substitute mint or parsley

Dry-fry the sesame seeds in a small, non-stick pan, watching carefully that they don't burn!

Cut the tofu into little squares about 2 cm (¾ inch) square, 1 cm (½ inch) deep, and fry gently in the 15 ml spoon (1 tablespoon) vegetable oil with half the sesame seeds until golden. Put aside.

Sauté the chilli, garlic and onion in 1 x 15 ml spoon (1 tablespoon) olive oil until the onion turns translucent. Add the finely sliced fennel and the white wine (or apple juice or water) and stew for 10 minutes. Add the tomatoes and chickpeas, and sauté for another 5 minutes.

Meanwhile cook the pasta in plenty of salted, boiling water until it is 'al dente'. Drain, toss with the remaining spoon of oil, and then again with the vegetable sauce and the olives, and serve with the herbs, the tofu and the remaining toasted sesame seeds sprinkled on top.

59 Basic Italian tomato sauce

This Italian tomato sauce is based on the recipe from my second book, *Pastability: A Second Helping*. For a simpler, quicker version, see recipe 48 on page 106.

I love the Italian tomato sauces – they are not only the most delicious of all (when prepared the right way), but also the healthiest and least fattening as they contain no animal fat, just a little olive oil. I have been making the classic Italian tomato sauce, made with ingredients available in England, for some years now, and have to admit that the following recipe is perfection, as well as being simple to make (although it does have to simmer for quite a long time).

There are many optional variations in even this basic recipe. Tastes are individual; I like to include lots of chilli and garlic because I like spicy food, although in these recipes I have included just enough of these to make the dishes 'perky' without being too spicy. Feel free to adjust quantities or leave out ingredients altogether according to your taste.

As fresh Italian plum tomatoes are generally unavailable in Great Britain, I strongly recommend using the tinned variety rather than English tomatoes. I find carrots improve the flavour and texture of the sauce and add a pleasant slight sweetness, but if you have none in the house (or can't be bothered), they are optional.

As for herbs, I love oregano in tomato sauces but you might prefer to use dried thyme or sage, or fresh herbs from your garden. I would recommend sage or basil (1 x 15 ml spoon/1 tablespoon, finely chopped or cut up with kitchen scissors) or else marjoram and oregano in a slightly smaller quantity (a 10 ml dessert spoon), or else even thyme or rosemary in a smaller quantity still (a 5 ml teaspoon very *finely* chopped). Wine depends on availability; I would think twice about opening a bottle especially!

This recipe can be used as a basis for many sauces. I would suggest making a large quantity – perhaps double the amounts given here – and then freezing it in cup-size portions, so that you can run up a host of delicious pasta concoctions at a moment's notice.

For 3–4 main course or 6 starter helpings, use:

2 x 15 ml spoons (2 tablespoons) good olive oil
1 large onion (175 g/6 oz), finely sliced
1 small dried red chilli (1 cm/½ inch) to taste (optional)
2–4 cloves garlic, crushed
75–100 g (3 oz) carrots, coarsely grated (optional)
1 very large tin (800 g/1 lb 12 oz) Italian plum tomatoes,
  coarsely chopped
2 x 15 ml spoons (2 tablespoons) tomato purée
2 bay leaves
2 x 5 ml spoons (2 teaspoons) dried oregano, or 1 x 15 ml
  spoon (1 tablespoon) fresh chopped herbs
½ glass white wine (optional)
1 x 5 ml spoon (1 teaspoon) sugar, caster or granulated
salt and pepper
325 g (12 oz) quills, or any other sort of pasta

Sauté the onion in the olive oil with the chilli and half the garlic until the onion is translucent and softened. Add the carrots (if using) and sauté for a further couple of minutes. Add the tin of tomatoes, breaking up the fruit with a wooden spoon. Add the tomato purée, bay leaves, oregano, wine, sugar and seasoning, stir well, and then turn the heat up high. As soon as the sauce begins to bubble, stir it again, and turn the heat down very low. Simmer for an hour, stirring occasionally, and taking care not to let the sauce stick to the bottom of the pan or it will burn. Add the rest of the garlic about 10 minutes before the end of cooking. In a liquidiser or food processor, blend about three-quarters of the sauce until smooth. Mix together with the remaining quarter. Reheat gently at the last moment before adding to the pasta.

Meanwhile, cook the pasta in plenty of salted, boiling water until 'al dente'. Drain, and then put back into the pan, or into a preheated serving dish. Add the sauce, stir together well, and serve immediately with cheese on the side (if you feel you need it).

Fish Dishes
Quick and Easy

- Take trouble to make sure that you are cooking with enough water. If water goes cloudy, boil up a kettle and add more boiling water.

- If you think the pasta and sauce might turn out a little dry, some people suggest draining the pasta quickly and leaving in some of the cooking water.

- Instead of serving freshly grated Parmesan, try putting a lump of Parmesan and a grater on the table so people can grate their own.

- *Always* taste the pasta before adding grated cheese. It often doesn't need it, especially any pasta with fish, and that includes anchovies.

- Always feel free to *substitute*. That's what all the best Italian cooks do – they make the sauce with whatever is in the house, the garden or available that week in the market.

- Almost all my ingredients are optional, apart from the pasta itself! Experiment with what you have and what you like, and invent your own sauces, using my recipes as a base.

- The secret of a good tomato sauce is never burning the garlic. It should always retain its white colour. If the garlic goes crispy and brown, take it out and start again!

- Adjust the chilli according to taste. It is very hard to give an accurate measurement as chillies vary. The saying is, the smaller the hotter.

- Always remember to use lots and lots of fast-boiling, lightly salted water to cook your pasta.

- If your pasta is soggy and tasteless, or continues cooking after you have drained it, here are some possible reasons:

    You've overcooked it;

    You've used an unreliable brand. Use good-quality Italian pasta, for example, de Cecco or Barilla (not Buitoni) or experiment with your local supermarket produce until you find one that works well for you.

- If your pasta is soft on the outside but still hard in the centre it could be that you are not using enough water to cook it in.

- Find a brand of pasta that you like and stock up on it. I recommend F. lli de Cecco, Barilla (not Buitoni) and Marks and Spencer dried fresh egg pasta.

- If you use a good brand of pasta and cook it correctly (with lots of salted, boiling water until it is 'al dente') it will not go mushy on you – you can even drain it, toss it with a spoonful of oil and heat it up later or the following day.

- Feel free to experiment. Be brave. Open the fridge and make a sauce with whatever falls out.

- Stock up on store cupboard standbys from the Introduction and you will always be able to dish up a meal for friends at short notice.

- If you are partial to one of the spicy tomato sauces make extra and freeze in cupfuls. Add a little extra oil after defrosting.

- Buy herbs in pots at your local supermarket and keep them on your kitchen windowsill.

- Buy pesto sauce from the chilled section of the supermarket and freeze in ice cube trays. Decant into a plastic bag and keep frozen for future use.

- I heard Delia Smith the other day on television saying, 'Life is too short to roast a red pepper.' All I can say is I disagree – totally – and I am quite a lazy cook and believe in dishes that can be prepared quickly with the minimum amount of fuss. I *don't* find roasting red peppers a hardship. It's easy-peasy and quick. Just follow my instructions.

60 Spaghetti with smoked salmon and cream

Some fishmongers, delicatessens and even supermarkets sell smoked salmon offcuts at a reduced price, so this dish need not be as extravagant as it may seem.

For 4 starter size helpings, use:

100–175 g (4–6 oz) smoked salmon or smoked salmon trout pieces
275 ml (½ pint) single cream
225 g (8 oz) spaghetti (or spaghettini)
15 g (½ oz) butter
salt and pepper

Put the smoked salmon pieces into a bowl with the cream and set aside.

Cook the pasta in plenty of salted, boiling water until 'al dente'. Drain and put back into the pan over a very low heat with the butter and seasoning, stirring with a wooden spoon until the butter has melted. Strain the cream, now salmon-flavoured, into the pasta and allow it to heat through. Add the smoked salmon at the last moment before serving, to ensure it does not cook and go mushy, so losing its delicate and delicious quality.

61 Quills with smoked salmon, vodka and cream

This is a particularly delicious dish, simple and luxurious.

For 8 starter size helpings, use:

325–350 g (12 oz) smoked salmon (offcuts)
450 g (1 lb) quills
9 x 15 ml spoons (9 tablespoons) vodka
275 ml (½ pint) double cream
salt and pepper
1 x 15 ml spoon (1 tablespoon) chopped fresh dill
  (if available)

Cut the smoked salmon into small pieces and put aside.

Cook the pasta in plenty of salted, boiling water until 'al dente'. Drain and put back into the pan or a preheated serving dish. At the last moment, heat the vodka and cream until almost boiling. (Take care not to let it boil over as it might catch fire. This happened to me once – it was not serious, just surprising!) Mix the cream, vodka, smoked salmon, seasoning and dill into the hot pasta.

Serve immediately.

Note: All the above needs to be done extremely quickly, so that the pasta and sauce remain hot but the smoked salmon does not cook.

62 Quills or shells with avocado, lemon and optional shrimps or prawns

Simple and quick to make, this is a good dish for a party – you can make it even tastier, and prettier to look at, by adding a roast red pepper, sliced into little strips (see recipe 32, page 74 for instructions on preparation), or about 100–125 g (4 oz) French beans, steamed or boiled for just a few minutes so as to retain their crispness and colour.

This dish can be made leaving out the prawns or shrimps, especially if you are using a colourful vegetable.

For 3 main course or 6 starter size helpings, use:

   1 ripe avocado
   3 x 15 ml spoons (3 tablespoons) lemon juice
   1 clove garlic, crushed
   1 x 5 ml spoon (1 teaspoon) grainy or Dijon mustard
   150 ml (5 fl oz) single or double cream
   sea salt and freshly ground black pepper
   4 or 5 shakes of Tabasco sauce (to taste)
   125–175 g (4–6 oz) prawns or shrimps, precooked
   200–325 g (9–12 oz) quills or shells

Peel the avocado and cut into quarters, leaving one quarter with the stone (the stone is supposed to stop the avocado turning brown). Sprinkle this quarter with 1 x 15 ml (1 table-spoon) lemon juice and put aside for garnish at the end, cutting into slices just before adding to the pasta. Cut the other three quarters into chunks, put onto a large plate with the crushed garlic. Mash with a fork. Put the remaining lemon juice into a cup, add the spoon of mustard and the Tabasco and mix together well. Mash the lemon juice and mustard together with the avocado and garlic and then the cream. Season with the sea salt and black pepper. (You could combine these ingredients in either a liquidiser or food processor, but I find it almost easier to mash them by hand, unless you are making a large quantity.) At the last moment, heat the sauce gently with the shrimps or prawns in a double boiler. (As I don't possess one, I heat it in a small saucepan placed inside a larger one half full of water – as long as you make sure the water doesn't boil over into the sauce, this method works just fine!)

Meanwhile, cook the pasta in plenty of salted, boiling water until 'al dente', drain and put back into the pan, or into a preheated serving dish. Mix together with the sauce, and serve immediately on preheated plates, with the sliced pieces of reserved avocado scattered across the top. Serve extra Tabasco rather than cheese on the side.

63 Tagliatelle with smoked salmon, capers and cream

This recipe was given to me by oil baron, diplomat and great host Ricky di Portanova. Ricky and his wife Sandra live in great style, travelling between Acapulco, Houston in Texas and Claridge's in London, and dine in the finest restaurants in the world. However, every so often a longing for this particular dish seizes them, and Ricky orders the ingredients and a hotplate to be brought to the restaurant table, whereupon he prepares this delicious dish for his guests and himself.

An optional extra would be to garnish this dish with chopped parsley or fresh coriander, salmon eggs or even chopped, hard-boiled egg.

For 2 main course or 4 starter size helpings, use:

> 100–125 g (4 oz) smoked salmon, cut into pieces
> juice of ½ lemon
> sea salt and freshly ground black pepper
> 200 g (7 oz) egg tagliatelle (de Cecco, if you can find it)
> 1 generous 15 ml spoon (1 tablespoon) butter
> 150 ml (5 fl oz) single or thin double cream,
>   (or half and half of each)
> 4 x 15 ml spoons (4 tablespoons) capers, drained
> nutmeg, grated, to taste
> Swiss cheese (Emmenthal or Gruyère), grated

Cut up the salmon, using a sharp knife or kitchen scissors. (The smell of fish can be removed by later rubbing the scissors or knife blades with the used half-lemon.) Put on a plate and squeeze over a light sprinkling of lemon juice, and some black pepper.

Cook the pasta in plenty of salted, boiling water until 'al dente', drain and put back into the pan with the spoon of butter. Quickly heat the cream, watching it carefully and taking it off the flame just after it starts to boil. Add the capers. Toss the pasta with the butter until the butter has melted and coated the pasta. Pour on the capers and cream. Season with sea salt, a little more freshly ground black pepper, and a little grated nutmeg, and toss again. At the last moment before serving, mix in the salmon pieces, retaining a few to sprinkle on the top. Serve with freshly grated Swiss cheese on the side.

64 Tagliatelle with avocado, anchovies and black olives or herbs

This sauce has a pleasing, smooth texture which goes well with the tagliatelle, coating it all over and tinting it pale green. It is a good idea to include either the black olives and/or herbs – they add that important touch of extra flavour and colour; although the sauce is also exceptionally delicious on its own, served on spaghetti. Alternative additions would be red, or red and yellow roast peppers (see recipe 32, page 74 for instructions on preparation) or coarsely chopped, sun-dried tomatoes and some toasted pine kernels (see recipe 38, page 87). This would make a good starter for a dinner party as it looks impressive and interesting, tastes wonderful, and is extremely quick and easy to prepare.

Buying olives can be a risky business; some varieties, although large and interesting to the eye, are completely tasteless. I would recommend using the smallish kalamata black olives, which are always tasty.

For 2 main course or 4 starter size helpings, use:

1 large ripe avocado
5 anchovies
2–3 cloves garlic, crushed
½ dried red chilli, crumbled into tiny pieces (optional)
1 x 15 ml spoon (1 tablespoon) freshly squeezed lemon juice
3 x 15 ml spoons (3 tablespoons) olive oil
sea salt and freshly ground black pepper
225 g (8 oz) tagliatelle, or spaghetti
10 black olives, pitted and chopped into halves or thirds
  or 2 x 15 ml spoons (2 tablespoons) parsley, coriander or basil, finely chopped.

Peel the avocado and cut into quarters, leaving one quarter attached to the stone to prevent browning. Put aside for garnish at the end, cutting into slices just before adding to the pasta. Cut the other three quarters into chunks, put on a plate with the anchovy fillets and crushed garlic, and chilli (if using). Mash with a fork. Mash in the lemon juice (to taste) and then 2 of the spoons of olive oil. Season with the sea salt and black pepper.

Meanwhile, cook the tagliatelle or spaghetti in plenty of salted, boiling water until 'al dente'. Drain and put back into the pan with the remaining spoon of oil. Toss quickly over a low flame, add the sauce, and continue tossing the pasta in the sauce until the pasta is evenly coated. Put onto a preheated serving dish, or serve individually onto preheated plates. At the last moment sprinkle over the olives, herbs, sun-dried tomatoes or roast red pepper, and the sliced avocado pieces. Serve with chilli or Tabasco sauce on the side.

65 Bows with smoked trout, leeks and cream

The colours of this dish are pale and pretty, so you may want to serve a strongly coloured vegetable on the side – for example, steamed broccoli or a juicy mixed salad.

You may need to vary the amount of smoked trout, depending on what is available. One whole medium smoked trout will probably produce about 125–150 g (4–5 oz) of fillet. You could also substitute 100–125 g (4 oz) smoked salmon, thinly sliced and tossed together with the pasta and sauce just before serving. Keep the Tabasco bottle handy for those people who favour a little extra piquancy! And don't forget the lemon juice, it really brings out the flavour of the smoked trout.

For 2 main course or 4 starter size helpings, use:

> 175 g (6 oz) smoked trout fillets, chopped into 1 cm
>   (½ inch) pieces
> juice of ½ lemon
> salt and freshly ground black pepper
> 175 g (6 oz) leeks, sliced
> 4 x 15 ml spoons (4 tablespoons) double cream
>   *or* substitute 4 x 15 ml spoons (4 tablespoons) yoghurt
>   or crème fraîche for the cream
> 2 x 15 ml spoons (2 tablespoons) white wine or vermouth
>   (or substitute extra cream)
> pinch of nutmeg, finely grated, to taste
> 225 g (8 oz) bows or butterflies

Squeeze some lemon juice over the chopped trout fillets, followed by some freshly ground black pepper. Put on the side. Steam or parboil the leeks until softened. Drain well, then cook gently in the cream for a few minutes, adding the wine and nutmeg halfway through. Add the smoked trout and heat through well, just before adding to the cooked pasta.

Meanwhile, cook the pasta in plenty of salted, boiling

water until 'al dente', drain and put back in the pan. Add the sauce and heat gently over a low flame, mixing the pasta and sauce continuously, until heated through and well integrated. Serve immediately on well-heated plates with plenty of freshly ground black pepper, but no cheese!

66 Spaghettini with red caviar

Culinary expert *extraordinaire*, Loyd Grossman, invented this recipe for his book *The Millionaire's Diet Book* (published by Macdonald). Although terribly simple, it really hits the spot!

The red caviar is in fact red salmon roe, and not to be confused with the orange-red lumpfish roe, a vastly inferior (although considerably cheaper) product. The dish is delicious, unashamedly luxurious, non-fattening, and simplicity itself to prepare – well worth the extra expense and the trouble of finding a shop which sells the stuff!

Loyd recommends using one of the finer spaghettis, such as spaghettini, vermicelli or fedellini, preferably de Cecco.

For 4 starter or small main course helpings, use:

275 g (10 oz) spaghettini (or thin spaghetti)
100–125 g (4 oz) salmon roes (we use a brand called Keta)
15 g (½ oz) butter

Cook the pasta in plenty of salted, boiling water until 'al dente'. Drain, and put into a preheated serving dish with the butter. When the butter has melted, gently stir in the 'caviar' (salmon roe), using a wooden spoon.

Serve immediately.

67 Spaghetti with anchovies and mushrooms

This is a favourite with my family, all the more popular because not only is it quite delicious, it is also quick, simple and economical to prepare.

If you have the time it is worth making the effort to find really good mushrooms. I used some lovely ones called *'champignons marrons'* which I found at my local supermarket – they resemble a large and especially firm button mushroom, but are dark brown in colour. Another possibility would be to use large flat field mushrooms, if available – they are particularly tasty.

For 2 main course or 4 starter size helpings, use:

- 15 g (½ oz) butter *or* 2 x 15 ml spoons (2 tablespoons) olive or nut oil
- 75–100 g (3 oz) onions, finely sliced
- 1–2 cloves garlic, crushed
- 4 anchovy fillets, coarsely chopped
- 175 g (6 oz) mushrooms, finely sliced
- 4 x 15 ml spoons (4 tablespoons) white wine *or* substitute vegetable stock made with hot water and a pinch of vegetable stock cube or 1 x 5 ml (1 teaspoon) of vegetable bouillon powder *or* half sherry, half water
- sea salt and freshly ground black pepper
- 175 g (6 oz) spaghetti

Sauté the onions in the oil or butter until translucent and softened. Add the garlic and the anchovies and sauté for another couple of minutes, stirring with a wooden spoon. Add the mushrooms and then simmer, covered, for a further few minutes, stirring frequently, and adding the vegetable stock or wine after the first minute or so. Season to taste.

Meanwhile, cook the pasta in plenty of salted, boiling water until 'al dente', drain and then put back into the pan. Pour over the sauce, and heat through over a low flame, stirring continuously. Serve immediately, with cheese on the side only if your friends and relations clamour for it!

68 Linguini with tomatoes, anchovies, olives, capers and optional sun-dried tomatoes and pine kernels

This is one of my all-time favourites – spicy, healthy, easy to cook and pretty to look at – another dish that never fails to hit the spot! And, believe it or not, it's a store cupboard standby.

I have added optional sun-dried tomatoes and pine kernels – optional because, if you don't happen to have any in the larder, I wouldn't want to put you off making this absolutely delicious dish. Rather than leaving them out completely, you could, if you have these ingredients available, substitute strips of roast red pepper, or a spoonful of pesto, or sun-dried tomato *paste* instead of the sun-dried tomatoes, and chopped walnuts or pecan nuts in place of the pine kernels.

For 3 main course or 4–6 starter size helpings, use:

3 x 15 ml spoons (3 tablespoons) extra virgin olive oil
75–100 g (3 oz) onion (red, if available), finely chopped
1 small dried red chilli (approx. 3 cm/1 ¼ inches long),
   finely chopped
5 anchovy fillets, coarsely chopped
medium tin (400 g/14 oz) Italian plum tomatoes
2 ½ x 15 ml spoons (2 ½ tablespoons) tomato purée
2–3 cloves garlic, crushed
4 large green olives and 4 large black olives, pitted and
   coarsely chopped (or use 8 of either colour)
1 x 15 ml spoons (1 tablespoon) capers, drained
4 sun-dried tomatoes, chopped (optional)
350 g (12 oz) linguini or spaghetti
2 x 15 ml spoons (2 tablespoons) pine kernels (if available)

Sauté the onion in the oil with the chilli and anchovy fillets until the onion is translucent and softened. Add the tinned tomatoes, breaking them up with a wooden spoon. Turn up the heat and continue to cook, stirring very frequently and taking care not to let the sauce burn. After a few minutes add the tomato purée, garlic, olives, capers and sun-dried tomatoes and simmer, covered, stirring frequently for about another 10 minutes, or until the sauce thickens into a loose purée consistency. Season to taste.

Meanwhile, cook the pasta in plenty of salted, boiling water until 'al dente', drain and put into the pan with the sauce. Toss the pasta and sauce together over a low flame until heated through and well integrated. Sprinkle over the pine kernels, if using, and serve piping hot on preheated plates, with *no* cheese on the side!

More Fish Dishes

- Take trouble to make sure that you are cooking with enough water. If water goes cloudy, boil up a kettle and add more boiling water.
- If you think the pasta and sauce might turn out a little dry, some people suggest draining the pasta quickly and leaving in some of the cooking water.
- Instead of serving freshly grated Parmesan, try putting a lump of Parmesan and a grater on the table so people can grate their own.
- *Always* taste the pasta before adding grated cheese. It often doesn't need it, especially any pasta with fish, and that includes anchovies.
- Always feel free to *substitute*. That's what all the best Italian cooks do – they make the sauce with whatever is in the house, the garden or available that week in the market.
- Almost all my ingredients are optional, apart from the pasta itself! Experiment with what you have and what you like, and invent your own sauces, using my recipes as a base.
- The secret of a good tomato sauce is never burning the garlic. It should always retain its white colour. If the garlic goes crispy and brown, take it out and start again!
- Adjust the chilli according to taste. It is very hard to give an accurate measurement as chillies vary. The saying is, the smaller the hotter.
- Always remember to use lots and lots of fast-boiling, lightly salted water to cook your pasta.
- If your pasta is soggy and tasteless, or continues cooking after you have drained it, here are some possible reasons:

  You've overcooked it;

  You've used an unreliable brand. Use good-quality Italian pasta, for example, de Cecco or Barilla (not Buitoni) or experiment with your local supermarket produce until you find one that works well for you.
- If your pasta is soft on the outside but still hard in the centre it could be that you are not using enough water to cook it in.
- Find a brand of pasta that you like and stock up on it. I recommend F. Ili de Cecco, Barilla (not Buitoni) and Marks and Spencer dried fresh egg pasta.
- If you use a good brand of pasta and cook it correctly (with lots of salted, boiling water until it is 'al dente') it will not go mushy on you – you can even drain it, toss it with a spoonful of oil and heat it up later or the following day.
- Feel free to experiment. Be brave. Open the fridge and make a sauce with whatever falls out.
- Stock up on store cupboard standbys from the Introduction and you will always be able to dish up a meal for friends at short notice.
- If you are partial to one of the spicy tomato sauces make extra and freeze in cupfuls. Add a little extra oil after defrosting.
- Buy herbs in pots at your local supermarket and keep them on your kitchen windowsill.
- Buy pesto sauce from the chilled section of the supermarket and freeze in ice cube trays. Decant into a plastic bag and keep frozen for future use.
- I heard Delia Smith the other day on television saying, 'Life is too short to roast a red pepper.' All I can say is I disagree – totally – and I am quite a lazy cook and believe in dishes that can be prepared quickly with the minimum amount of fuss. I *don't* find roasting red peppers a hardship. It's easy-peasy and quick. Just follow my instructions.

69 Spaghetti with anchovies, olives, tomatoes and capers

This is my version of a traditional Italian dish known as 'Spaghetti alla putanesca', which translates roughly as 'Roman whore's spaghetti'. Why it is so called I don't know, but certainly the dish *could* be described as spicy and satisfying . . .

Again, it is an excellent store cupboard standby, if you can remember to keep a stock of the basic ingredients handy.

You can serve grated Parmesan on the side, though the Italians generally feel that cheese should not be used on any pasta dish containing fish. Of course, if you are a strict vegetarian, you may prefer to make this dish leaving out the anchovies.

For 2 main course helpings use

2 x 15 ml spoons (2 tablespoons) olive oil
2 cloves garlic, crushed
8 anchovy fillets, coarsely chopped
up to ¼ x 5 ml spoon (up to ¼ teaspoon) chilli powder
    or 1 small fresh or dried red chilli (to taste)
16 black olives, halved and pitted
1 x 5 ml spoon (1 teaspoon) dried oregano
1 x 15 ml spoon (1 tablespoon) capers, drained of vinegar
    and coarsely chopped
salt and pepper
325 g (12 oz) fresh tomatoes, skinned, *or* tinned tomatoes
1 x 15 ml spoon (1 tablespoon) tomato purée
3 x 15 ml spoons (3 tablespoons) fresh, chopped herbs
    (e.g. parsley, basil, sage or coriander, if available)
225 g (8 oz) spaghetti (or spaghettini)

Put the oil, crushed garlic and anchovies into a large saucepan and cook over a low heat until the anchovies disintegrate into the oil. Stir in the chilli, and then add the olives, dried oregano, capers, seasoning and finally the tomatoes. Simmer over a low heat for 25 minutes, stirring every few minutes and adding some water or vegetable stock if the sauce appears to be drying up. Add the fresh herbs (if used) during the cooking.

Meanwhile, cook the pasta in plenty of salted, boiling water. Drain the moment it is 'al dente' and put back into the pan. Pour the sauce on top, and cook for a couple of minutes to allow the pasta to absorb some of the tomato sauce.

Serve very hot.

70 Frank's spaghetti vongole

A really excellent (and very easy) version of an all-time Italian classic, this was created by an American friend, Frank McEvitt.

For 4 main course helpings, use:

25 g (1 oz) butter
1 x 15 ml spoon (1 tablespoon) oil
100–125 g (4 oz) onions, finely sliced (if possible, use the dark red onions)
5 cloves garlic, crushed
450–575 g (16–20 oz) tinned baby clams
4 fl oz/125 ml (1 wine glass) white wine
25 g (1 oz) fresh, chopped parsley
salt and pepper
450 g (1 lb) spaghetti (or spaghettini))

Melt the butter with the oil in a large frying pan or saucepan. Add the onions and garlic and sauté until the onions are translucent. Stir in the clam juice and the wine, and boil briskly until the liquid has reduced by about half. Add the clams and heat through for less than a minute. The parsley and seasoning should be added to the sauce at the last minute.

Meanwhile, cook the pasta in plenty of salted, boiling water. Drain and put into a preheated serving dish. Mix the sauce well into the pasta.

Serve immediately.

71 Spaghetti with tuna, tomatoes, anchovies and olives

This dish is extremely tasty, easy to prepare and another good 'store cupboard standby'.

For 6–8 starter size or 4 main course helpings, use:

3 x 15 ml spoons (3 tablespoons) olive oil
1 large clove garlic, crushed
100–125 g (4 oz) onions, finely sliced
2 pinches chilli powder, to taste (optional)
3 anchovy fillets, coarsely chopped
10 olives (preferably black), halved and pitted
185 g (6½ oz) tin tuna fish, drained
2 x 15 ml spoons (2 tablespoons) white wine
400 g (14 oz) tinned Italian tomatoes
1 x 15 ml spoon (1 tablespoon) tomato purée
1 x 5 ml spoon (1 teaspoon) dried oregano
150 ml (¼ pint) vegetable stock (fresh, or made with ¼ stock cube), or water
450 g (1 lb) spaghetti or rigatoni

In a large frying pan sauté the garlic and onion in the oil over a low heat. Stir in the chilli powder, if used. After a minute, stir in the anchovies, and continue to sauté until they have disintegrated. Add the olives, tuna fish and white wine, stirring together continuously with a wooden spoon and the tomato purée. Next add the tomatoes, breaking them up with the spoon. Season, then cover the pan and simmer on a low heat for 30 minutes. (Cooking for this length of time enriches the flavour, though if you are very short of time you could shorten it.) Every 5 minutes or so, remove the lid from the pan to stir the sauce and to add the vegetable stock (or water), bit by bit.

Meanwhile, cook the pasta in plenty of salted, boiling water until 'al dente'. Drain the pasta, then return it to the pan and toss with the sauce. Serve immediately.

72 Spaghetti Machiavelli with king prawns, mushrooms, chilli, garlic and basil

Machiavelli is a restaurant in the heart of Sydney's business centre, decorated with villainous-looking mug shots of some of Australia's more eminent politicos. To me, it is the ideal Italian *trattoria*: large, friendly, noisy, and serving heaped helpings of rustic fare which, for abundance, flavour and freshness would shame most of its lackadaisical international counterparts. In the middle of the restaurant, Giovanna Toppi presides over a huge wooden table laden with antipasto: bowls of red peppers and Mozzarella, olives, omelettes, 20-kilo Parmesan cheeses, and a cornucopia of salad. Over this fantastic still-life is suspended a 'chandelier' of whole prosciuttos, salamis and mortadellas. Shirt-sleeved lunchers can glance into the open-plan kitchen and observe Giovanna's daughter Paola nonchalantly tossing the *'specialità della casa'* – an exquisite seafood pasta – in an enormous, spitting frying pan while, across the room, her chicly attired sister writes the 'dockets'.

Paola explained that in Italy, where the butter is strangely white and tasteless, this dish would be made with oil, and she taught me a trick for preparing sauces which don't have much 'base'. She strains the pasta quickly and not too thoroughly, leaving in a little of the salted water in which the pasta was cooked. This adds just the necessary extra amount of liquid.

For 3 main course or 6 starter size helpings, use:

12 king prawns (cooked)
325–350 g (12 oz) spaghetti
6 x 15 ml spoons (6 tablespoons) butter
1 x 15 ml spoon (1 tablespoon) olive oil
3–4 cloves garlic, crushed
4 anchovies, chopped
1–2 small red chillies (fresh or dried), to taste, finely sliced
sea salt and freshly ground black pepper

175 g (6 oz) mushrooms, finely sliced

30 fresh basil leaves, torn into halves, *or* substitute 2 x 15 ml spoons (2 tablespoons) fresh parsley or coriander, finely chopped, *or* 1 x 10 ml spoon (1 dessertspoon) oregano, dried

Peel the king prawns and then split in half, de-veining at the same time.

Cook the spaghetti in plenty of salted, boiling water until 'al dente'.

Whilst the pasta is cooking, put all the remaining ingredients (except about a quarter of the fresh herbs) into a large frying pan, and sauté over a medium heat for about 2 minutes. Put aside until the pasta is ready.

Drain the pasta, allowing a little of the cooking water to remain, and put back into the pan. Meanwhile, gently reheat the seafood and mushroom sauce, add to the pasta, and then toss quickly over a medium heat until the pasta and sauce are well integrated and heated through. Put onto a preheated serving dish, or serve individually onto preheated plates. Sprinkle over the remaining fresh herbs and then serve immediately.

73 Linguini with tomato and seafood

An excellent, strong and spicy seafood pasta, special enough to serve at a dinner party as either a starter or a main course. If you cannot find any one of the fish ingredients, substitute with something similar or increase the quantities of the other fish. Serve with a big mixed salad and cheese to follow.

For 5–6 main course or 7–9 starter size helpings, use:

- 3 x 15 ml spoons (3 tablespoons) olive oil
- 175 g (6 oz) onion (red, if available), finely sliced
- 4 cloves garlic, crushed
- 2 small dried red chillies (approx. 3 cm/1¼ inches long each), finely chopped
- 5 anchovy fillets
- 175 g (6 oz) squid, ready cleaned and sliced
- 1 medium carrot (about 75–100 g/3 oz) grated
- 1 very large tin (794 g/1 lb 12 oz) Italian plum tomatoes
- 2 x 15 ml spoons (2 tablespoons) tomato purée
- ¾ wine glass red or white wine
- 1 x 5 ml spoon (1 teaspoon) dried thyme
- 6 black olives, pitted and chopped
- 2 x 15 ml spoons (2 tablespoons) capers
- 3 x 15 ml spoons (3 tablespoons) butter
- 175 g (6 oz) monkfish, or other firm white fish, cut into small chunks
- 100–125 g (4 oz) prawns, precooked and shelled
- 100–125 g (4 oz) cockles, precooked and shelled
- 100–125 g (4 oz) mussels, precooked and shelled
- 400–500 g (15–18 oz) linguini, spaghetti, or quills

Sauté the onions in the olive oil until translucent and softened. Add two of the cloves of crushed garlic, the chillies and the anchovy fillets, and sauté for another minute or so. Add the squid and sauté for a further couple of minutes, then add the carrot and sauté for another minute or two. Add the tin of tomatoes, breaking them up with a wooden spoon. Add the tomato purée, wine, and thyme, and turn up the heat until the sauce bubbles. Give it a good stir, put the lid on and simmer for about an hour on a medium heat, stirring every so often and taking care not to let the ingredients burn or stick to the bottom of the pan. About 10 minutes before the sauce has finished cooking, throw in the olives and drained capers.

Sauté the monkfish and the prawns in a separate pan with half the butter and a clove of crushed garlic until the monkfish is more or less cooked – opaque white. Put in the pan with the tomato and squid. Sauté the cockles and mussels for just half a minute or so with the remaining butter and clove of crushed garlic. At the last moment, add to the sauce and heat through.

Meanwhile, cook the pasta in plenty of salted, boiling water until 'al dente'. Drain and put into a preheated serving dish. Mix in a couple of tablespoons of olive oil, and pour on the well-heated sauce. Mix together, and serve immediately on preheated plates.

74 Rigatoni with creamy crab, tomato, avocado and sage

This recipe is not as long and complicated as it may seem at first glance. In essence, I am suggesting using the recipe for quills with crab and creamy tomato sauce (recipe 78, page 160) with a spicy avocado mixture. It's a good way of using up a slightly over-ripe avocado.

For 6 starter size or 3–4 main course helpings, use:

1 x 15 ml spoon (1 tablespoon) olive oil
2 cloves garlic, crushed
1 medium-size dried chilli (to taste), chopped
400 g (14 oz) tomatoes (fresh or tinned), coarsely chopped
½ x 5 ml spoon (½ teaspoon) sugar
1 x 5 ml spoon (1 teaspoon) dried oregano
250 g (9 oz) tinned crab
6 x 15 ml spoons (6 tablespoons) single cream

For the avocado mixture
1 ripe medium/large avocado
4 anchovies (optional)
6 shakes Tabasco sauce or ½ x 5 ml spoon (½ teaspoon) chilli powder
2 cloves garlic, crushed
1 x 15 ml spoon (1 tablespoon) oil
2 x 15 ml spoons (2 tablespoons) fromage frais, single cream, or plain yoghurt
300–400 g (12–14 oz) rigatoni or quills

For the garnish
about 10 leaves fresh sage, chopped (or substitute fresh basil or coriander)
50 g (2 oz) toasted pine kernels (optional)
1 lemon, sliced into quarters

To make the basic sauce

Sauté the garlic and the chilli in the oil for about 30 seconds, and then throw in the tomatoes, sugar and oregano. Simmer on a low heat for about 15 minutes, stirring frequently, or until the sauce begins to take on a jam-like consistency. Strain as much brine as you can out of the tinned crab and add to the sauce. Add the cream and stir (gently) together.

To make the avocado mixture

Peel the avocado, slice coarsely and put onto a plate or chopping board. Mash together with the anchovies (if using), Tabasco, crushed garlic, oil, sea salt and pepper. Slide off the plate into a small bowl and stir in the fromage frais, cream or yoghurt.

Meanwhile, cook the pasta in plenty of salted, boiling water until 'al dente'. Then drain the pasta and return it to the pan. Add the crab and tomato cream sauce and the avocado mixture, and toss together over a low flame.

Serve immediately, with the pine kernels (see recipe 38 on page 87 for instructions on preparation) and sage (or basil) leaves sprinkled on the top, and a quarter of lemon on the side of each plate.

75 Twists with anchovies, grilled tomatoes and cream

This dish is surprisingly delicate in flavour and colour. Excellent as a starter, it can also be served as a main course with a big mixed salad to give the meal colour. Try it also with wholewheat pasta.

For 4 starter size helpings, use:

4 anchovy fillets
225 g (8 oz) fresh tomatoes
3½ x 15 ml spoons (3½ tablespoons) olive oil
1 x 5 ml spoon (1 teaspoon) dried oregano
salt and pepper
2 cloves garlic, crushed
8 x 15 ml spoons (8 tablespoons) single cream
225 g (8 oz) twists

Soak the anchovy fillets in a little milk. Cut the tomatoes in half and sprinkle with ½ x 15 ml (½ tablespoon) of the oil, the oregano and some salt. Grill until soft, then skin the halves and chop coarsely.

Chop the anchovies coarsely, and sauté gently with the garlic in the remaining olive oil – taking care not to let the garlic burn – until the anchovies disintegrate. Pour the cream into the pan and continue to cook until the cream begins to bubble. At this point stir in the chopped tomatoes and seasoning.

Meanwhile, cook the pasta in plenty of salted, boiling water until 'al dente'. Drain, and put into the pan containing the sauce. Continue to cook over a gentle heat for a minute or so until the sauce is well mixed with the pasta.

Serve immediately, *without* putting grated cheese on the table. Cheese would spoil the delicate taste of this dish.

76 Shells with scallops, cream and curry

A delicious and luxurious dish that is very simple and quick to make. It is excellent as a starter for a dinner party, or as a quick supper for two. (Instead of using scallops only, you could use a combination of scallops and prawns or shrimps.)

For 4 starter size helpings, use:

    25 g (1 oz) butter
    175 g (6 oz) scallops (with or without coral), cut into small
      pieces
    1/2–3/4 x 5 ml spoon (1/2–3/4 teaspoon) curry powder
    125 ml/4 fl oz (1 wine glass) white wine
    150 ml (1/4 pint) double cream
    225 g (8 oz) shells
    salt and pepper

Melt the butter in a large frying pan and gently sauté the scallops for a minute or so. Stir in the curry powder. Add the wine, and allow to bubble until the liquid has reduced by about half. Then stir in the cream.

Meanwhile, cook the pasta in plenty of salted, boiling water until only just 'al dente'. Remove quickly from the heat, drain and put into the pan with the sauce. Continue cooking the pasta and sauce over a low heat, stirring with a wooden spoon, until the pasta is fully cooked and has absorbed some of the liquid from the sauce.

Serve immediately, with ground black pepper but *no* cheese!

77 Spaghetti with salmon, cream and tarragon

Absolutely delicious, this is really one of my favourites, and very simple to make. I like the colours of this dish, the pink of the salmon and the dark green of the tarragon against the pasta and it is easily good enough to serve as a starter at a dinner party.

Use fresh, not dried, tarragon. I buy a cellophane packet from my local supermarket and use most of it, pulling the leaves away from the stalk and then chopping them coarsely.

You could also make this recipe using leftover salmon instead of fresh.

For 2 main course or 4 starter size helpings use:

20 g (¾ oz) butter
1 large salmon steak (at least 150 g/5 oz)
2 x 15 ml spoons (2 tablespoons) tarragon, chopped
3 x 15 ml spoons (3 tablespoons) white wine
125 ml (4 fl oz) double or single cream
175–225 g (6–8 oz) spaghetti

Remove the skin from the salmon, cut it into 6 pieces, removing the biggest bone, and sauté with the chopped tarragon very gently in the butter for a few minutes in the bottom of a medium-sized frying pan. Remove from the heat, transfer the salmon from the pan to a plate, and break into smaller-sized chunks, removing any remaining bones. Put back into the pan and pour over the wine and the cream. At the last moment, sauté again for minute or so – *very* gently – so as not to break up the salmon.

Meanwhile, cook the pasta in plenty of salted, boiling water until 'al dente', drain and return to the pan. Pour over the salmon and sauce, and serve immediately.

78 Quills with crab and creamy tomato sauce

Very easy to make and very rich, so I would serve this as a starter. I used the tinned cherry tomatoes, but it would work just as well with fresh cherry tomatoes, or ordinary tinned Italian tomatoes. If you have no pine kernels or basil, serve without, or substitute parsley or coriander just for the 'green' .

For 4 starter size helpings, use:

  1 x 15 ml spoon (1 tablespoon) olive oil
  2 cloves garlic, crushed
  1 medium-size dried chilli (to taste), chopped
  4 anchovies, well-drained and chopped (optional)
  400 g (14 oz) tomatoes (fresh or tinned), coarsely chopped
  ½ x 5 ml spoon (½ teaspoon) sugar
  1 x 5 ml spoon (1 teaspoon) dried oregano
  250 g (9 oz) tinned crab
  6 x 15 ml spoons (6 tablespoons) single cream
  300–400 g (12–14 oz) quills
  100 g (4 oz) toasted pine kernels (optional)
  About 12 leaves fresh basil (optional)
  1 lemon, sliced into quarters

Sauté the garlic, chilli and anchovies (if using) in the oil for about 30 seconds, and then throw in the tomatoes, sugar and oregano. Simmer on a low heat for about 15 minutes, stirring frequently, or until the sauce begins to take on a jam-like consistency. Strain as much brine as you can out of the tinned crab and then add to the sauce. Add the cream and stir together.

Meanwhile, cook the pasta in plenty of salted, boiling water until 'al dente'. Then drain the pasta and return it to the pan. Add the crab and tomato cream sauce, and toss together over a low flame.

Serve immediately, with the toasted pine kernels
(see recipe 38, page 87) and basil leaves (if using) sprinkled
on the top, and a quarter of lemon on the side of each plate.

79 Salmon, spinach, leek, mushroom and tarragon lasagne

This is another useful lasagne, very tasty, and handy for entertaining. It's also a good way to use up leftover salmon.

You could experiment with an alternative sauce to pour over; for example, substituting a pesto sauce thinned down with some extra olive oil for the tarragon and cream sauce.

Serve with a big mixed salad full of crunchy leaves and with a good vinaigrette (see recipe 104, page 221).

For 6 main course helpings, use:

For the salmon filling
450 g (1 lb) salmon steak (275 g (10 oz) if weighed without skin and bones)
1 x 15 ml spoon (1 tablespoon) butter
1 x 15 ml spoon (1 tablespoon) chopped tarragon
1 x 15 ml spoon (1 tablespoon) lemon juice
salt and pepper

For the spinach filling
500 g (18 oz) leaf spinach (fresh or frozen)
1 x 15 ml spoon (1 tablespoon) butter
1 clove garlic
salt and pepper
3 x 15 ml spoons (3 tablespoons) single or double cream
¾ x 5 ml spoon (¾ teaspoon) grated nutmeg
zest of ½ a lemon

For the mushroom and leek filling
2 x 15 ml spoons (2 tablespoons) butter
2 cloves garlic
200 g (7 oz) mushrooms, washed, or peeled and finely sliced
450 g (1 lb) leeks (250 g (10 oz) if weighed trimmed), carefully washed and finely sliced

For the béchamel sauce
30 g (1½ oz) butter
30 g (1½) flour
575 ml (1 pint) milk
1 x 5 ml spoon (1 teaspoon) mustard powder

For the sauce to pour over the lasagne
25 g (1 oz) butter
2 or 3 x 15 ml spoons (2–3 tablespoons) tarragon
6 x 15 ml spoons (6 tablespoons) crème fraîche, or cream,
    or crème fraîche and cream mixed
½ x 5 ml spoon (½ teaspoon) nutmeg

Additional ingredients
325–350 g (12 oz) lasagne
75 g (3 oz) grated Parmesan or Emmenthal or half of each
    cheese
salt and pepper

Wrap the salmon in foil parcels with the butter, tarragon, lemon juice and some salt and pepper, and bake in a preheated oven on a medium heat (190°C/375°F/gas mark 5) for about 30 minutes. Remove from the foil parcels (retaining the juices). Remove the skin and bone (if necessary). Put on a plate and break into big flakes following the natural divisions of the fish. Pour over the juices and put aside.

If you are using frozen spinach, defrost it in a very little boiling, salted water. Strain, pushing the spinach against the strainer or colander to remove as much liquid as possible. If the spinach is fresh, cook it in a very little milk, strain, and chop coarsely. Toss in a pan over a low heat with the butter and crushed garlic. Season and then stir in the cream, grated nutmeg and lemon zest.

For the mushroom and leek filling, sauté the garlic and the mushrooms in the 2 x 15 ml spoons (2 tablespoons) butter until softened. Add the leeks and continue to sauté until the leeks are well softened (4–5 minutes), adding a little liquid (water or vegetable stock if required). Be careful not to add too much liquid or allow any of the fillings to become too liquid or you will end up with a slushy lasagne.

Cook the lasagne as instructed on page 6. Make the béchamel sauce (page 224).

Take a shallow ovenproof dish, no more than 8 to 10 cm (3 or 4 inches) deep and about 38 cm (15 inches) by 25.5 cm (10 inches) – I use an attractive oval earthenware dish which I can bring to the table. Oil the bottom of the dish. Spread a layer of lasagne across the bottom, followed by a layer of salmon and spinach. Follow this with a thin layer of béchamel and a light sprinkling of Parmesan cheese, salt and pepper. Now spread a double layer of the lasagne. Next add a layer of the leek and mushroom mixture and again follow this with the béchamel, Parmesan cheese and salt and pepper. Carry on with these layers until you run out of ingredients. (This takes a little bit of prejudgement. You might decide that you have enough of each filling ingredient to make two layers of each or maybe only one, or maybe the third layer will combine the salmon spinach filling with the leek and mushroom filling.) End with a good layer of béchamel and a good sprinkling of the grated cheese.

Cover the dish with foil, and bake in a fairly hot oven (200°C/400°F/gas mark 6) for 1–1½ hours. Remove the foil for the last 15–20 minutes to allow the cheese topping to brown.

Serve the sauce in a small jug on the side, or else pour over each portion.

80 Twists with smoked salmon, red peppers, chives, pine kernels, cream and vodka

This recipe was given to me by a New Zealand friend, Catherine Bolus. She's a *wonderful* cook with movie star looks.

For 5–6 main course or 8–10 starter size helpings use:

½ x 15 ml spoon (½ tablespoon) olive oil
2 red peppers
salt and pepper to taste
500 g (1 lb) dried twists (or other shape pasta if wanted)
100 g (3 oz) pine nuts
500 ml (1 pint) single cream
9 x 15 ml spoons (9 tablespoons) vodka
1 garlic clove, crushed
200 g (7 oz) smoked salmon
1–2 x 15 ml spoons (1–2 tablespoons) chives, chopped
  (optional)
2 x 15 ml spoons (2 tablespoons) Parmesan, grated
extra grated Parmesan to serve (optional)

Place the whole red pepper on the grill pan, with the pepper nearly touching the heating element, and grill under a high heat. (Most of the skin will turn black but will peel off to reveal an unburnt, delicious pepper underneath.) Remove from the grill, cool slightly and peel, then cut the peeled pepper into strips and lay on a plate. Dribble the ½ x 15 ml spoon (½ tablespoon) of olive oil over the strips, and sprinkle with a little salt and pepper. Leave for a few minutes, then slice into smaller pieces.

Dry-fry the pine kernels in a non-stick pan, turning constantly until they are lightly roasted.

Meanwhile, cook the pasta in plenty of salted, boiling water until 'al dente'. Drain and return to the pan.

Bring the cream, vodka and garlic up to the boil, then take off the element and add smoked salmon, chives, red pepper, Parmesan, salt and pepper. Put the pasta into a serving bowl, pour the cream mixture over, toss lightly and then sprinkle the toasted pine nuts over the top and serve.

Note: Work fast and be careful not to let the smoked salmon sit in the hot cream for more than a few seconds or it will cook.

81 Arabella Boxer's smoked haddock and tagliatelle pie

The first cook book I was ever given was *First Slice Your Cook Book* by Arabella Boxer, a brilliant collection of very useful recipes in a book which was sliced into three sections: the first third of each page was a starter, the second third a main course recipe and the last third a dessert. Thus you could have the recipes for the whole meal laid out at once on the page.

This recipe was one of my favourites, particularly handy as it comprised the whole main course at once and you could prepare it all in advance – essential for entertaining on one's own. I would serve it with a big crunchy salad and my mother's wonderful cold lemon soufflé for dessert.

The addition of pasta is not in the original recipe, but I find it works magically well. For a variation, sprinkle toasted pine kernels or chopped herbs (chives or tarragon) over the top. Or if you cannot find any decent tomatoes, then substitute a serving of basic tomato sauce (see recipe 59, page 125) for the fresh tomatoes.

For 4–6 main course helpings, use:

   2 large smoked haddock fillets, de-boned and skinned,
      or substitute 500 g (1 lb) smoked cod
   4 eggs
   6 medium to large tomatoes (450 g/1 lb)
   675 g (1½ lb) spinach *or* 2 large packets (500 g) frozen
      leaf spinach
   1 x 15 ml spoon (1 tablespoon) butter
   1 or 2 cloves garlic, crushed (optional)
   pinch or two grated nutmeg, to taste (optional)
   275–325 g (10–12 oz) tagliatelle (dried) or any of the
      Marks and Spencer 'fresh egg pasta' range
   1 x 15 ml spoon (1 tablespoon) olive oil
   75–100 g (3 oz) freshly grated Parmesan
   or substitute 100–125 g (4 oz) grated Cheddar or Gruyère

For the béchamel sauce

30 g (1½ oz) butter
30 g (1½ oz) flour
1 x 5 ml spoon (1 teaspoon) mustard powder
50 g (2 oz) grated cheese (Parmesan, Cheddar or Gruyère)
575 ml (1 pint) milk

Bring a large pan of water to the boil. Cut the fish into 8 pieces. When the water boils, put in the fish, cover and remove from the heat. After 10 minutes, drain and cool fish. Remove the skin and bone, and flake it.

Hard-boil the eggs. Cool, shell and slice thickly. Peel the tomatoes after dipping in boiling water, and slice them.

Cook the spinach and drain, forcing out all the water with a wooden spoon. Toss over a low heat with the spoonful of butter and the garlic and nutmeg (if using).

Meanwhile, cook the pasta in plenty of salted, boiling water until 'al dente'. Drain and return to the pan.

Make the béchamel sauce, following the directions on page 224.

Butter a large soufflé dish. Put the spinach in the bottom of the dish, then a layer of pasta, followed by a thin layer of the béchamel and a sprinkling of the cheese. Next put in the flaked fish, the sliced eggs and then another layer of pasta followed by the tomatoes (or tomato sauce). Pour over the remaining béchamel sauce and shake gently (but well) to make sure the sauce penetrates. Sprinkle over the remaining cheese and then bake in a slow oven for 40 minutes. Keep the dish hot for an hour or two until you are ready to serve it or, if necessary, reheat gently.

Oriental Vegetable Dishes

- Take trouble to make sure that you are cooking with enough water. If water goes cloudy, boil up a kettle and add more boiling water.

- If you think the pasta and sauce might turn out a little dry, some people suggest draining the pasta quickly and leaving in some of the cooking water.

- Instead of serving freshly grated Parmesan, try putting a lump of Parmesan and a grater on the table so people can grate their own.

- *Always* taste the pasta before adding grated cheese. It often doesn't need it, especially any pasta with fish, and that includes anchovies.

- Always feel free to *substitute*. That's what all the best Italian cooks do – they make the sauce with whatever is in the house, the garden or available that week in the market.

- Almost all my ingredients are optional, apart from the pasta itself! Experiment with what you have and what you like, and invent your own sauces, using my recipes as a base.

- The secret of a good tomato sauce is never burning the garlic. It should always retain its white colour. If the garlic goes crispy and brown, take it out and start again!

- Adjust the chilli according to taste. It is very hard to give an accurate measurement as chillies vary. The saying is, the smaller the hotter.

- Always remember to use lots and lots of fast-boiling, lightly salted water to cook your pasta.

- If your pasta is soggy and tasteless, or continues cooking after you have drained it, here are some possible reasons:

    You've overcooked it;

    You've used an unreliable brand. Use good-quality Italian pasta, for example, de Cecco or Barilla (not Buitoni) or experiment with your local supermarket produce until you find one that works well for you.

- If your pasta is soft on the outside but still hard in the centre it could be that you are not using enough water to cook it in.

- Find a brand of pasta that you like and stock up on it. I recommend F. lli de Cecco, Barilla (not Buitoni) and Marks and Spencer dried fresh egg pasta.

- If you use a good brand of pasta and cook it correctly (with lots of salted, boiling water until it is 'al dente') it will not go mushy on you – you can even drain it, toss it with a spoonful of oil and heat it up later or the following day.

- Feel free to experiment. Be brave. Open the fridge and make a sauce with whatever falls out.

- Stock up on store cupboard standbys from the Introduction and you will always be able to dish up a meal for friends at short notice.

- If you are partial to one of the spicy tomato sauces make extra and freeze in cupfuls. Add a little extra oil after defrosting.

- Buy herbs in pots at your local supermarket and keep them on your kitchen windowsill.

- Buy pesto sauce from the chilled section of the supermarket and freeze in ice cube trays. Decant into a plastic bag and keep frozen for future use.

- I heard Delia Smith the other day on television saying, 'Life is too short to roast a red pepper.' All I can say is I disagree – totally – and I am quite a lazy cook and believe in dishes that can be prepared quickly with the minimum amount of fuss. I *don't* find roasting red peppers a hardship. It's easy-peasy and quick. Just follow my instructions.

82 Green Thai aubergine coconut curry

I'm usually put off using aubergines because they seem to drink up so much oil in the cooking, which boosts the calories in the dish! In this dish, however, we steam them first, which softens them beautifully without adding a single calorie.

This is a vegetarian version of the famous Thai green coconut curry. It is a very subtle dish – a delicate grey, with the seeds and the black slices of aubergine skin producing a decorative and pleasing effect. As with all the coconut curries, it is quite rich, and people who have never eaten Thai food might find the taste a little unusual.

Use either Chinese egg noodles, or noodles made from rice (see page 10).

For 2 main course or 4 starter size helpings, use:

1 large aubergine (225–275 g/8–10 oz)
    or 275 g (10 oz) round green aubergines
300 ml (10 fl oz) tinned coconut milk
1 x 15 ml spoon (1 tablespoon) nut or vegetable oil
1 clove garlic, crushed
1 spring onion, finely sliced
1 x 5 ml spoon (1 teaspoon) green curry paste
1 x 15 ml spoon (1 tablespoon) fresh root ginger, grated or
    finely chopped
3 kaffir lime leaves, finely slivered with scissors
½ x 5 ml spoon (½ teaspoon) palm sugar *or* substitute one
    generous teaspoon thick honey or sugar
150 g (5 oz) Chinese egg noodles, or rice sticks
2 x 15 ml spoons (2 tablespoons) fresh coriander,
    chopped (optional)

Cut the aubergine into thick slices, sprinkle with a little salt and leave on a kitchen towel to drain. After 10 minutes turn the slices and leave them for another 10 minutes. Steam for a few minutes until soft. Cool, then chop coarsely.

Pour the coconut milk into a bowl and beat with a fork or spoon until the creamy part is well integrated with the thinner liquid.

Sauté the garlic and spring onion in the oil in the bottom of a medium-sized saucepan over a low heat for just a few seconds. Add the curry paste and continue to stir until mixed together with the oil. Add the steamed and chopped aubergine, then the coconut milk and stock (or water), and stir together well, still over a low flame. Add the ginger, lime leaf, and palm sugar, and stir together. Simmer for a minute or two then stew on a low flame for about 10 minutes, taking care not to let it burn.

At the last moment, cook the Chinese noodles in plenty of salted, boiling water for just a couple of minutes, taking great care not to overcook. (If you are using rice sticks, prepare as described on page 10). Mix together gently with the sauce on a preheated dish, sprinkle over the chopped coriander, and serve immediately.

83 Vegetarian red coconut curry, served with noodles

The red curry has a slightly saltier flavour than the green. If you look at the list of ingredients for these two curries in a Thai cook book, you will see that the green is made with green chillies, red with red, but apart from that there seems to be not much difference!

Again, a delicate Thai-style curry that goes equally well with noodles or rice.

For 2 light main course helpings, use:

300 ml (10 fl oz) tinned coconut milk
1 x 15 ml spoon (1 tablespoon) nut or vegetable oil
1 clove garlic, crushed
1 x 15 ml spoon (1 tablespoon) red curry paste
1 x 15 ml spoon (1 tablespoon) fresh root ginger, grated or finely chopped
2.5 cm (1 inch) galangal, peeled and sliced into thin rounds
½ x 15 ml spoon (½ tablespoon) fish sauce (optional)
3 whole kaffir lime leaves, finely slivered using kitchen scissors
2 inches lemon grass, finely sliced
1 x 5 ml spoon (1 teaspoon) palm sugar *or* substitute one generous teaspoon thick honey or sugar
275 g (10 oz) small round green aubergines, halved, *or* 275 g (10 oz) Mediterranean aubergines, slices cut into quarters
½ red pepper (or yellow or green), finely sliced
a little water or vegetable stock
225 g (8 oz) courgettes, sliced
150 g (5 oz) Chinese egg noodles

Pour the coconut milk into a bowl and beat with a fork or spoon until the creamy part is well integrated with the thinner liquid. Measure out the 225 ml (8 fl oz).

Sauté the garlic in the oil in the bottom of a medium-sized

saucepan over a low flame for just a few seconds. Add the curry paste, and stir until mixed together with the oil. Add the coconut milk and stir together well, still over a low flame. Add the ginger, galangal, fish sauce (if using), lime leaves, lemon grass and palm sugar, and stir together. Simmer for a minute or two, then add the aubergine and pepper. Cover and simmer for 5 minutes, until the aubergine softens and reduces in volume, then add the courgettes. Simmer on a very low heat for another 20 minutes, stirring occasionally, and taking care not to let the sauce burn, adding a little stock or water if necessary.

At the last moment, cook the Chinese noodles in plenty of salted, boiling water for just a couple of minutes, taking great care not to overcook. Drain and then mix gently with the sauce on a preheated dish and serve immediately, or serve separately with noodles (or rice) on the side.

84 Spicy Thai spring greens with kaffir lime leaves and coconut milk

You could actually make this recipe with almost any leafy green vegetable – for example, Savoy cabbage, spinach or even with courgettes. Spring greens, however, have a particularly individual and strong taste which seems to combine well with these other ingredients, and when available they are usually one of the best buys around.

For 2 light main course helpings, use:

275 g (10 oz) spring greens, sliced into medium/fine strips
1½ x 15 ml spoon (1½ tablespoons) nut or vegetable oil
1–2 cloves garlic, crushed
1 large spring onion, finely sliced
1 x 5 ml spoon (1 teaspoon) fresh root ginger, grated or
    finely chopped
3 kaffir lime leaves, finely slivered with scissors
½ x 5 ml spoon (1 teaspoon) palm sugar *or* substitute one
    generous teaspoon thick honey or sugar
1 x 5 ml spoon (1 teaspoon) fish sauce (optional)
5 cm (2 inches) lemon grass, finely sliced
125 ml (4 fl oz) tinned coconut milk
a little stock or water
150 g (5 oz) Chinese egg noodles, buckwheat
    or 'soba' noodles

Steam or boil the sliced spring greens for a few minutes until softened. Sauté the garlic and spring onion in the oil in the bottom of a medium-sized saucepan over a low flame for just a few seconds. Add the ginger, lime leaves, palm sugar, fish sauce, lemon grass, coconut milk, and spring greens, and continue to sauté for about 5 minutes, adding a little vegetable or chicken stock, or water mixed with coconut milk, if the mixture becomes too dry.

At the last moment, cook the Chinese noodles in plenty of

salted, boiling water for just a couple of minutes, taking great care not to overcook. Drain, and then mix together gently with the sauce on a preheated dish, and serve immediately.

85 Thai fried rice noodles ('Pad Thai') with bean sprouts, peanuts and coriander

My version of my friend Sandy Forsyth's recipe for a Thai classic – Pad Thai.

I have added some soy sauce, kaffir lime leaves and lemon grass to the original recipe, as I found the dish rather on the bland side without. If you want to be truly *authentic*, then omit those ingredients.

Sandy suggests all ingredients should be prepared in advance and put into small (ramekin-style) dishes. Once you have prepared your ingredients, then the whole process of cooking this dish should take no longer than three minutes. Use dried 'Sen Lek Noodles' (a flat rice flour noodle sold at the Thai shops).

This dish will serve two people as a modest main course serving. However, if you are combining it with other dishes (for example, one or two of the Thai coconut curries described in this book) then it will go a lot further. Four of us ate this dish for lunch, together with a big plate of steamed courgettes tossed in a little sesame seed oil, crushed garlic and with a few toasted sesame seeds sprinkled on top. We drank lemon grass and ginger tea (see the introduction to recipe 93 on page 197 for instructions on how to make this).

Sandy recommends using a wooden spatula as a spoon will tend to break up the rice noodles. These spatulas are available in Chinese shops in Soho, in Thai shops, and from Habitat.

For 3–4 main course helpings, use:

50 g (2 oz) peanuts, ready shelled
225 g (8 oz) Sen Lek noodles or rice sticks
3 x 15 ml spoon (3 tablespoons) vegetable or nut oil
3 cloves garlic, crushed
2 eggs
3 spring onions, finely sliced

Additional ingredients

1 chilli (to taste), finely chopped or crumbled

2 kaffir lime leaves (cut out the spine and then cut the halved leaves into slivers)

7.5 cm (3 inches) lemon grass, very finely sliced

1 x 15 ml spoon (1 tablespoon) fresh ginger root, grated

100–125 g (4 oz) bean sprouts

1 x 15 ml spoon (1 tablespoon) lime juice (if not available, substitute lemon juice)

1 x 15 ml spoon (1 tablespoon) fish sauce

2 x 15 ml spoons (2 tablespoons) soy sauce (mixed with 1 x 15 ml spoon [1 tablespoon] water) *or* 3 x 15 ml spoons (3 tablespoons) light soy sauce

1 x 5 ml spoon (1 teaspoon) palm sugar, or white sugar

2–3 x 15 ml spoons (2–3 tablespoons) fresh coriander, coarsely chopped

125 ml (4 fl oz) vegetable stock (or water)

Roast the peanuts on a baking tray in a medium to high oven for 15–20 minutes or until they begin to darken in colour and become crisper. Remove from the oven, allow to cool and then remove the husks. Put them in a plastic bag and then crush them using a rolling pin or with a pestle and mortar.

Soak the noodles in cold water for 20 minutes. Drain. At the last minute before adding to the dish, pour boiling water over them, leave for 20 seconds or so. Drain again.

Stir-fry half the garlic in half the oil for just a few seconds, taking great care it doesn't burn (turn brown and bitter). Break in the eggs and stir rapidly for a few seconds. Add noodles and stir well, scraping down sides with the wooden spatula. Slice onto a serving platter, cover and keep warm.

Stir-fry the remaining garlic, the chilli and the spring onions in the remaining oil for about 30 seconds or until the spring onions soften.

Add the kaffir lime leaves, lemon grass and ginger; stir; and then add the bean sprouts, lime juice, fish sauce, soy sauce, palm (or white sugar), half the peanuts and half the coriander. Stir-fry until the bean sprouts soften.

Now transfer the cooked noodles back into the wok and toss together with the other cooked ingredients, adding some of the water, vegetable stock (or chicken stock if you're not a strict vegetarian). Put back onto the serving plates and sprinkle over the remaining peanuts and coriander.

Serve immediately.

86 Thai spring rolls filled with bean thread (or rice vermicelli), vegetables, coriander and kaffir lime leaves

I prefer these to the comparatively boring Chinese spring rolls. At first I was terrified at the prospect of deep-frying, but actually it was relatively easy. I bought a huge bottle of sunflower oil, and used the wok. Because of its shape it seems to use less oil than a heavy saucepan. However, you might feel a saucepan is more stable sitting on a hob.

Deep-frying is always a fire hazard, so be very careful, keep children away and make sure you have a fire extinguisher or fire blanket not too far away.

For about 14–16 rolls (7 starter size helpings) use:

100–125 g (4 oz) bean thread noodles or rice vermicelli
1 x 15 ml spoon (1 tablespoon) vegetable
     or sesame seed oil
4 medium/large spring onions, including green part (or
     shallots), finely sliced
1 large clove garlic, crushed
1 red chilli
1 x 15 ml spoon (1 tablespoon) fresh ginger root, finely
     chopped or grated
3 kaffir lime leaves, finely slivered with scissors
50 g (2 oz) red pepper, finely sliced
50 g (2 oz) mushrooms, finely sliced
100–125 g (4 oz) Chinese or Savoy cabbage, finely sliced
175 g (6 oz) tinned crab, drained of its brine (optional)
1 egg, beaten
2 x 15 ml spoons (2 tablespoons) light soy sauce
3 x 15 ml spoons (3 tablespoons) chopped fresh coriander
     leaves
1/2–1 x 15 ml spoon (1/2–1 tablespoon) fish sauce
1 x 5 ml spoon (1 teaspoon) sugar

4 x 15 ml spoons (4 tablespoons) coconut milk (or substitute vegetable stock)

about 16 large sheets of spring roll pastry (available ready made)

vegetable oil for deep-frying

Soak the noodles in cold water for about 15–20 minutes. At the last minute, before adding to the other ingredients, drop them into a pan or bowl of boiling water, leave for about 30 seconds and drain in a colander or sieve. Chop the noodles (whilst still in the colander) with kitchen scissors to make them more manageable.

Stir-fry the spring onion, garlic, chilli, ginger and kaffir lime leaves in the oil, until the spring onion starts to soften and darken in colour. Add the red pepper and mushrooms and stir-fry for 30 or 40 seconds, or until they start to soften. Add the cabbage and again stir-fry for 30 or 40 seconds or until it starts to soften. Add the crab (if using), stir-fry for another 10 seconds and then add the cooked noodles and stir-fry again. Throw on the egg and stir-fry briskly as it cooks. Throw on the light soy sauce, fish sauce, sugar, coconut milk and the coriander. Turn over a few more times.

Fill the spring roll pastry sheets, following the directions on the back of the packet.

Deep-fry (in the wok) in very hot oil until crispy. Serve immediately with sweet red chilli dipping sauce (also available from Thai shops) on the side.

87 Cold soba noodles, Japanese-style

My version of a handy soba recipe, taken from my friend Mr Tony Lim's 'classic chilled soba'. Tony Lim used to be chef at one of Melbourne's most interesting vegetarian restaurants, 'The Shaka-hari', in Lyon Street, Carlton.

For 2 starter size helpings, use:

- 125 g (4 oz) dried soba noodles
- 1/4 sheet nori (seaweed)
- 4 pieces wood ear fungus, soaked in warm water for 30 minutes, sliced into eights (optional)
- 2 spring onions, finely chopped
- 150 g (5 oz) fresh tofu or bean curd
- 1 x 15 ml spoon (1 tablespoon) toasted sesame seeds

For the sauce
- 1 x 15 ml spoon (1 tablespoon) sesame seed oil or vegetable oil
- 2 x 15 ml spoons (2 tablespoons) light soy or tamari or half dark soy, half water
- 2 x 5 ml spoons (2 teaspoons) ginger, peeled and grated finely
- 1 x 15 ml spoon (1 tablespoon) mirin, sake, white wine or apple juice
- 1/2 x 15 ml spoon (1/2 tablespoon) vegetable oil
- 1/2 x 5 ml spoon (1/2 teaspoon) sugar, or to taste

Toast the sesame seeds over a low heat in a non-stick pan, turning almost continuously with a wooden spoon.

In a medium- to large-sized saucepan, bring water to the boil. Add the noodles and bring the water back to the boil again. Cook the noodles until just tender, no more than 3–5 minutes. Drain and rinse in cold water. Drain again in a colander.

Meanwhile, toast the sheet of nori over a naked flame until

it turns bright green and/or crisps up. Cut into fine shreds. Combine the sauce ingredients in a screw-top jar and give it a few good shakes.

Place the noodles in a mixing bowl. Add the sauce, wood ear fungus and chopped spring onions. Toss gently.

Divide the noodles into four serving bowls. Scatter the cubed tofu, sesame seeds and nori on top. Serve immediately.

88 Japanese buckwheat noodles with shitake and oyster mushrooms, ginger, courgettes, black and white sesame seeds, tofu and nori (toasted seaweed) or coriander

Japanese food is pricey, but then their attitude to food is entirely different. They believe in eating a small quantity of *perfect* food: the best quality, freshest ingredients beautifully presented, rather than large amounts of an inferior product. They regard with horror the overflowing plates of messy foodstuffs, filled with dairy produce consumed by us Westerners. Apparently, to the Japanese, we give out the aroma of cheese, thanks to all the milk, cheese and butter in our diets.

So, therefore, the quantities may seem smaller than you are used to. The solution is simple: eat out of a smaller bowl, using chopsticks if possible. Remember, it takes 20 minutes for the message to reach your stomach from your brain that you've eaten . . . which accounts for one of the reasons why so many of us carry on eating after our body's nutritional requirements have been met.

Once, in a Japanese restaurant, I found a little leaflet on which were written three golden rules of Japanese chefs. As far as I can remember they were roughly as follows:

Respect for the quality of your ingredients, the privilege of cooking and preparing these exquisitely perfect foods.

Respect for all the knowledge and skills of cooking that have come down to you from the grand masters of cooking, and which you are privileged to be able to apply to your work.

A humble attitude; every time you cook a dish it should be as if for the first time, with the same enthusiasm, concentration and freshness of attitude.

The following recipe is not, to my knowledge, a classic Japanese dish but something I put together combining several different ideas.

Mr Tony Lim suggests using 'nori' in his classic soba noodle recipe, which I have used as a basis for my recipe on page 182. He suggests 'toasting a sheet of "nori" over a flame until it turns bright green'. My attempts to hold my sheet of nori over the naked gas flame resulted in almost instant fire. I blew it out and only then noticed that the nori was already – I suppose – a fairly respectable shade of green. Perusal of the packet revealed that *my* nori was ready toasted!

I was called away to the phone immediately after draining the buckwheat noodles. When I returned, they were a congealed mass in the strainer. I dumped the whole lot into a saucepan and, luckily, the addition of the 'half the sauce' and a little gentle prodding with a wooden spoon (in the pan) over a low flame restored the noodles to sanity.

For 2 main course or 3 starter size helpings, use:

For the sauce

  1 x 5 ml spoon (1 teaspoon) sesame seed oil
  2 x 15 ml spoons (2 tablespoons) light soy
  1½ x 5 ml spoons (1½ teaspoons) mirin or sake, or white wine, or Martini and water
  1½ x 5 ml spoons (1½ teaspoons) caster sugar

Additional ingredients

  1 x 15 ml spoon (1 tablespoon) sesame seed oil
  1 x 15 ml spoon (1 tablespoon) vegetable or nut oil
  1 large clove garlic, crushed
  ½ chilli, crushed
  1 x 15 ml spoon (1 tablespoon) fresh ginger, grated
  4 spring onions, finely sliced
  100–125 g (4 oz) shitake and/or oyster mushrooms, sliced
  100–125 g (4 oz) courgette (yellow, if you can find one), cut into half lengthwise, then finely sliced
  100–125 g (4 oz) bean curd (tofu), cubed
  ½ sheet nori (Japanese seaweed), shredded, *or* substitute chopped coriander leaves
  150 g (5 oz) Japanese buckwheat (soba) noodles

3 x 15 ml spoons (3 tablespoons) sesame seeds, toasted
1 x 15 ml spoon (1 tablespoon) black sesame seeds
   (optional)

Mix together the sauce ingredients in a small bowl and put aside.

Using the wok or a large non-stick frying pan, stir-fry the garlic, chilli, fresh ginger and spring onions in the sesame seed and other oil until softened.

Add the mushrooms and courgettes and continue to stir-fry until *they* soften. Add the cubes of tofu, *half* the shredded seaweed and half the sauce and stir-fry again for about 30 seconds.

Meanwhile, cook the buckwheat noodles according to the directions on the packet (or, as with pasta, in plenty of lightly salted, boiling water until 'al dente'). Drain and put back into the pan with the remaining half of the sauce and *black* seeds (if using).

Slide the cooked buckwheat noodles onto a preheated serving dish, pour/distribute over the vegetables and sauce. Sprinkle over the sesame seeds and remaining shredded seaweed. Serve warm or hot.

89 Buckwheat noodles (or spaghettini) with ginger, soy sauce, orange, tofu and toasted sesame seeds

Very easy and quick – especially nice if you're partial to Japanese tastes.

For 2 starter size helpings, use:

   2 x 15 ml spoons (2 tablespoons) sesame seeds
   1 x 15 ml spoon (1 tablespoon) sesame seed oil (*or* substitute vegetable or nut oil)
   120 g (4 oz) firm tofu
   1 large clove garlic, crushed (optional)
   1 small dried chilli, to taste (optional)
   2 x 15 ml spoons (2 tablespoons) soy sauce
   4 x 15 ml spoons (4 tablespoons) orange juice
   2 x 5 ml spoons (2 teaspoons) honey
   1 x 15 ml spoon (1 tablespoon) fresh ginger root, grated
   1 x 15 ml spoon (1 tablespoon) fresh coriander, chopped (optional)
   125 g (4 oz) soba or buckwheat noodles, *or* spaghettini

Dry-fry the sesame seeds in a small, non-stick pan until golden brown, watching carefully to make sure that they don't burn.

Cut the tofu into squares, about 2 cm (¾ inch) square, 1 cm (½ inch) deep and fry gently in the sesame seed oil with the crushed garlic and chilli (if using) and half the toasted sesame seeds until golden. Put aside.

Heat the soy sauce with the orange juice, honey and ginger.

Meanwhile, cook the pasta in plenty of salted, boiling water until 'al dente'. Drain, put back in the pan and pour over the soy, orange, honey and ginger sauce. Toss over a gentle heat until well heated through.

Serve with the tofu squares, remaining sesame seeds and coriander (if using) sprinkled on top.

Oriental Fish Dishes

- Take trouble to make sure that you are cooking with enough water. If water goes cloudy, boil up a kettle and add more boiling water.
- If you think the pasta and sauce might turn out a little dry, some people suggest draining the pasta quickly and leaving in some of the cooking water.
- Instead of serving freshly grated Parmesan, try putting a lump of Parmesan and a grater on the table so people can grate their own.
- *Always* taste the pasta before adding grated cheese. It often doesn't need it, especially any pasta with fish, and that includes anchovies.
- Always feel free to *substitute*. That's what all the best Italian cooks do – they make the sauce with whatever is in the house, the garden or available that week in the market.
- Almost all my ingredients are optional, apart from the pasta itself! Experiment with what you have and what you like, and invent your own sauces, using my recipes as a base.
- The secret of a good tomato sauce is never burning the garlic. It should always retain its white colour. If the garlic goes crispy and brown, take it out and start again!
- Adjust the chilli according to taste. It is very hard to give an accurate measurement as chillies vary. The saying is, the smaller the hotter.
- Always remember to use lots and lots of fast-boiling, lightly salted water to cook your pasta.
- If your pasta is soggy and tasteless, or continues cooking after you have drained it, here are some possible reasons:

    You've overcooked it;

    You've used an unreliable brand. Use good-quality Italian pasta, for example, de Cecco or Barilla (not Buitoni) or experiment with your local supermarket produce until you find one that works well for you.
- If your pasta is soft on the outside but still hard in the centre it could be that you are not using enough water to cook it in.
- Find a brand of pasta that you like and stock up on it. I recommend F. lli de Cecco, Barilla (not Buitoni) and Marks and Spencer dried fresh egg pasta.
- If you use a good brand of pasta and cook it correctly (with lots of salted, boiling water until it is 'al dente') it will not go mushy on you – you can even drain it, toss it with a spoonful of oil and heat it up later or the following day.
- Feel free to experiment. Be brave. Open the fridge and make a sauce with whatever falls out.
- Stock up on store cupboard standbys from the Introduction and you will always be able to dish up a meal for friends at short notice.
- If you are partial to one of the spicy tomato sauces make extra and freeze in cupfuls. Add a little extra oil after defrosting.
- Buy herbs in pots at your local supermarket and keep them on your kitchen windowsill.
- Buy pesto sauce from the chilled section of the supermarket and freeze in ice cube trays. Decant into a plastic bag and keep frozen for future use.
- I heard Delia Smith the other day on television saying, 'Life is too short to roast a red pepper.' All I can say is I disagree – totally – and I am quite a lazy cook and believe in dishes that can be prepared quickly with the minimum amount of fuss. I *don't* find roasting red peppers a hardship. It's easy-peasy and quick. Just follow my instructions.

90 Bows with salmon (or bean curd), sugar snap peas (or green beans) and sesame seeds

A very special, very tasty meal for two. It is easily expandable into a really superb dish for serving at a dinner party, if you don't mind doing some cooking at the last minute. Multiply the ingredients accordingly, and mix up a little extra sauce (soy sauce, mirin and sugar, as below, with some chopped spring onion, heated up in a pan and served in a small jug on the side). You might even consider adding some slivered nori (Japanese seaweed – see recipes 87 and 88, on pages 182 and 184). This dish is especially suitable for those partial to the Japanese Teriyaki taste.

If you don't eat fish, then you could consider making this dish substituting 175 g (6 oz) bean curd or tofu for the salmon. Make sure that it is the *firmest* bean curd or tofu that you can find, so that it keeps its slices nicely when you fry it in the oil. Cut it into pieces about 4 cm (1½ inches) square and about 2 cm (¾ inch) thick.

I like to make this dish using Marks and Spencer's 'Fiorelli' in their fresh egg pasta range.

For 2 main course helpings, use:

  2 small fresh salmon fillets (about 75–100 g/3 oz each)
     or 175 g (6 oz) bean curd (tofu)
  2 x 15 ml spoons (2 tablespoons) sesame seed oil
  ½ a small dried chilli, chopped (to taste)
  2 medium-sized spring onions, finely chopped
  1 small clove garlic, crushed (optional)
  2 x 15 ml spoons (2 tablespoons) mirin, *or* sake, *or* white
     wine, *or* vermouth, *or* half sherry, half water
  2 x 15 ml spoons (2 tablespoons) soy sauce
     (or light soy sauce)
  1 x 5 ml spoon (1 teaspoon) caster sugar
  2 x 15 ml spoons (2 tablespoons) toasted sesame seeds

150 g (5 oz) sugar snap peas, trimmed *or* mange-tout,
   or even green beans
100–125 g (4 oz) bows (or quills)
2 x 15 ml spoons (2 tablespoons) fresh coriander,
   chopped (optional)

Toast the sesame seeds over a low heat in a non-stick pan,
turning almost continuously with a wooden spoon. (As with
pine kernels, you only have to turn your back for a second to
end up with charred, bitter remains.)

Gently fry the salmon fillets (or tofu) in the sesame seed oil
with the chilli, spring onions and garlic – if using – until
cooked to your taste. Some people like to leave the salmon a
little rare in the centre, whilst others prefer to cook it
through. If you're going to leave it rare, make sure the fillets
are *really* fresh. Then add the white wine, soy sauce and sugar
and half the toasted sesame seeds and cook for another half
minute or so.

Meanwhile, drop the sugar snap peas, mange-tout or green
beans into lightly salted, boiling water for a couple of minutes
until just slightly softened, but removing before they have a
chance to lose their fresh green colour. (Green beans will probably take longer, maybe 7 or 8 minutes.) I take the easy way
out and just drop them into the pasta water when it boils,
removing them with a slotted spoon *before* adding the pasta.

Meanwhile, cook the pasta in plenty of salted, boiling water
until 'al dente'. Then drain the pasta and return it to the pan.
Toss for a minute with a little extra sesame seed oil, and then
divide into portions and put onto the preheated plates.

Lay the salmon fillets and sugar snap peas on top and then
pour over the juices from the pan. Serve immediately, with the
remaining sesame seeds (and coriander, if using) sprinkled
over the top.

91 Thai green curry with salmon (or white fish), courgettes, aubergines, ginger, noodles and coriander

This pale green Thai 'curry' sauce is, in my experience, the most exquisite and universally popular of all Thai tastes. It *is* possible to make these curry pastes yourself, but I prefer to use the bought curry paste with the addition of a few key authentic (and fresh) ingredients from the Thai shop.

Pea aubergines are green, almost as small as peas, with a slightly peppery taste. Not one of the essentials of Thai cuisine, but very nice in this dish, if you can get hold of some. Both these and the round green aubergines are usually available at Thai provision stores. Remember that the pea aubergines and round small aubergines are optional. Apart from anything else, they are not always available, even in the best of Thai grocery shops. If you are *not* using them, then you don't need to cook the sauce for so long – about 10 minutes will do, just enough to infuse the ingredients.

I recommend making the salmon version of this dish. Not only do the flavours go well together, but the pink of the salmon looks quite spectacular against the pale green of the curry and herbs.

In the white fish version, the fish is cooked carefully in the oven in order to retain clearly discernible pieces of fish *with* sauce rather than allowing it to deteriorate into a mush! When I cooked the white fish version of this dish for some friends, one of them actually mistook the succulent chunks of this comparatively inexpensive cut of haddock for scallops!

I would serve this with some strongly coloured stir-fried or steamed vegetables – for example, broccoli, spinach, courgettes – and, if possible, some miniature corn on the cobs. It would go equally well with a plate of Basmati rice as with pasta.

For 3–4 main course helpings, use:

300 ml (10 fl oz) tinned coconut milk
½ x 15 ml spoon (½ tablespoon) green curry paste
1 clove garlic, crushed
1 x 15 ml spoon (1 tablespoon) nut or vegetable oil
    (for salmon version, 1 extra 15 ml spoon (1 tablespoon)
    nut, vegetable or, best of all, sesame seed oil)
2 x 15 ml spoons (2 tablespoons) fresh root ginger, grated
1 x 15 ml spoon (1 tablespoon) fish sauce (optional)
1 x 15 ml spoon (1 tablespoon) galangal, finely chopped
5 kaffir lime leaves, finely slivered with scissors
5 cm (2 inches) lemon grass, finely sliced
about 20 pea aubergines (optional)
1 x 5 ml spoon (1 teaspoon) palm sugar *or* substitute one
    generous teaspoon thick honey or sugar
100–125 g (4 oz) small round *green* aubergines, halved
    (optional)
175 g (6 oz) courgettes, sliced
350 g (12 oz) salmon, or firm white fish, e.g. haddock or
    cod (weighed without skin)
225 g (8 oz) Chinese egg noodles
2–4 x 15 ml spoons (2–4 tablespoons) fresh coriander,
    chopped

Open the tin of coconut milk and decant into a bowl. Beat
the contents with a fork or spoon until the cream part is well
integrated with the thinner liquid. Measure out the 300 ml
(10 fl oz) into another small bowl. Put aside.

Put the curry paste with the garlic and the oil in the bottom
of a pan and stir over a low heat until the paste is well mixed
with the oil. Stir in the coconut milk. Add the ginger, fish
sauce (if using), galangal, lime leaves, lemon grass, pea
aubergines (if available) and palm sugar, and stir together.
Simmer over a low heat for 5 minutes, and then add the
larger aubergines, simmer for another 15 minutes and then
add the courgettes. Cook for another 5 minutes.

If the fish has not already been skinned by the fishmonger,

then skin it yourself. Lay it on a chopping board with the skin downwards, against the board. Hold the thin/tail end in your left hand, and slice *away* from yourself, using the leverage against the board to remove the fish from the skin as cleanly as possible.

If using the salmon

Remove skin, if necessary (see above), and then cut the salmon into small chunks about 2 cm (¾ inch) square. At the last moment, sauté in a pan in the extra sesame or nut oil (1 x 15 ml/1 tablespoon) until *just* cooked – not too long or the fish will dry up. (Or bake in tin foil, see recipe 79, page 162.)

Meanwhile, cook the Chinese noodles in plenty of salted, boiling water for just a few minutes, watching them carefully, until done (remembering to stir well at the onset to separate the noodles). Drain. Put the noodles onto a flat, preheated serving dish. Pour the sauce over the noodles and then distribute the salmon chunks evenly on top. Sprinkle with the chopped coriander leaves, and serve immediately. Alternatively, serve separately, with noodles or rice on the side.

If using the white fish

Put the fish in a shallow, ovenproof dish just large enough to hold it and the sauce. Pour the sauce over, and cook in a preheated oven (190°C/375°F/gas mark 5) for about 15 minutes, until the fish is cooked, but not overcooked!

Meanwhile, cook the Chinese noodles in plenty of salted, boiling water for just a few minutes, watching them carefully, until done (remembering to stir well at the onset to separate the noodles). Drain. Put the noodles onto a flat, preheated serving dish. Slide the fish and sauce over the top. Break up the fish gently with a wooden spoon in order to distribute it fairly, but not to destroy the quality of the fish, sprinkle with the chopped coriander leaves, and serve immediately. Alternatively, serve separately, with noodles or rice on the side.

92 Thai red curry with white fish, prawns, crushed peanuts and noodles

Cook as for recipe 91, Thai green curry with salmon (or white fish), courgettes, aubergines, ginger, noodles and coriander, substituting 1 x 15 ml spoon (1 tablespoon) red curry paste for the green curry paste, and 100–125 g (4 oz) cooked and shelled prawns or shrimps for the courgettes, and replacing the chopped coriander with 50 g (2 oz) crushed, roasted peanuts, sprinkled over the dish just before serving.

Serve as recipe 91, with noodles, or serve separately, with noodles (or rice) on the side.

Note: Remember that the pea aubergines and the small, round aubergines are optional. Apart from anything else, they are not always available, even in the best of Thai grocery shops. If you are *not* using them, then you don't need to cook the sauce for so long – about 10 minutes will do, just enough to infuse the ingredients.

93 Ba mee nah talay (Thai fresh egg noodles with seafood)

My friend Sandy Forsyth is the most *brilliant* cook I know, especially when it comes to Oriental food – and I don't offer such praise lightly! She is married to Freddie Forsyth, the supreme master of the political thriller genre. Sandy gives marvellous Sunday lunch parties at their farm just outside London – with massive plates of fresh seafood, cooked in a wok, bowls of aromatic Thai noodles and green curries, huge salads of rocket and tomatoes fresh from the garden, all finished off with a Grand Marnier 'bombe'. This feast is eaten in the rose garden under the watchful eyes of two fox terriers, a Burmese cat, eight miniature goats and a magnificent American Bronze pet turkey called Stradivarius, who joins in the laughter with a turkey cackle or two. The following recipe is a wonderful example of Sandy's inventive brilliance.

Ba mee noodles are yellowy brown and are sold in packets in Oriental stores. Don't be put off by the several exotic ingredients in this recipe. It is well worth a trip to the Thai shop – and whilst you are there, stock up on extra ingredients, such as kaffir lime leaves which you can store in the deep-freeze, fresh lemon grass and ginger. These last three can be made into an exquisite lemon grass and ginger tea:

Chop up two or three lemon grass stalks with 2 or 3 knobs of ginger. Bruise with a meat pounder or rolling pin and then simmer in a saucepan with a few cups of water until the tea darkens to a pale amber.

When I first made this ba mee noodles recipe I left out the squid (unfortunately, it went 'off' after only 36 hours in the fridge). I used 100 g (4 oz) fresh prawns and substituted a tin of (John West) crabmeat (170 g) for the fresh crab and squid. I can tell you, no one complained!

For 2–3 main course size helpings, use:

1 red pepper
1 x 5 ml spoon (1 teaspoon) sesame seed oil (optional)
1 pack of ba mee noodles (about 450 g/1 lb)
4 x 15 ml spoons (4 tablespoons) vegetable, nut or sesame
    seed oil
3 cloves garlic, crushed
1 small chilli (dried or fresh), finely sliced
6 x 15 ml spoons (6 tablespoons) soy bean sauce (less
    potent than soy and sweeter)
or substitute 3 x 15 ml spoons (3 tablespoons) soy sauce, 3
    x 15 ml spoons (3 tablespoons) mirin (sake or white
    wine) and 2 x 5 ml spoons (2 teaspoons) sugar
or substitute 6 x 15 ml spoons (6 tablespoons) light soy
    sauce and 2 x 5 ml spoons (2 teaspoons) sugar
2 spring onions, finely sliced
6 kaffir lime leaves, finely sliced
1 x 5 ml spoon (1 teaspoon) grated ginger
scant half wine glass full wood ear mushrooms (wood
    fungus – Hed Hunu), when reconstituted they look jelly-
    like, *or* substitute 100 g (4 oz) shitake or oyster
    mushrooms or both mixed together, sliced
100–125 g (4 oz) raw prawns, peeled
100–125 g (4 oz) fresh crabmeat (white/brown, whatever
    your preference, but don't substitute crab sticks!)
100–125 g (4 oz) baby squid/octopus, cut into delicate
    rings (optional)
2 x 15 ml spoons (2 tablespoons) fish sauce
about 6 x 15 ml spoons (6 tablespoons) vegetable stock*
75–100 g (3 oz) tinned water chestnuts, sliced (the only
    vegetable that remains crisp when cooked)
2 x 15 ml spoon (2 tablespoons) fresh coriander, chopped

Place the whole red pepper on the grill pan, with the pepper
nearly touching the heating element, and grill under a high
heat. (Most of the skin will turn black but will peel off to

*If you are not a strict vegetarian then do consider using chicken stock.

reveal an unburnt, delicious pepper underneath.) Remove from the grill, cool slightly and peel, then cut the peeled pepper into strips and lay on a plate. Chop coarsely and dribble over the sesame seed oil (if using).

Take the noodles out of their packet, shake to loosen and then dip into boiling water and strain immediately, putting a tea cloth or kitchen paper under the colander.

In a hot wok add 2 x 15 ml spoons (2 tablespoons) of the oil and half the garlic and sauté (don't burn it!) until brown. Add the noodles and red pepper slices and then stir gently with a wooden spoon, pouring on half the soy bean sauce, or half the light soy sauce or soy sauce mixture and sugar. Put on a warm serving plate and cover with foil.

Heat the remaining oil with the garlic and the chilli in the wok, add the spring onions, mushrooms, kaffir lime leaves and grated ginger, stir-fry until softened, and then add the seafood, starting with the raw stuff, ending with the crabmeat and sliced water chestnuts. Add the soy bean sauce (or remaining light soy sauce or soy sauce and sugar), fish sauce, and vegetable stock.

Ladle over the noodles and serve immediately with the coriander leaves sprinkled on the top.

94 Bean thread or rice vermicelli stir-fry with crab, coriander and kaffir lime leaves

Another of those recipes which really 'hits the spot'. This was inspired by watching Keith Floyd on television cooking fresh crab and bean thread noodles on the beach in Thailand. It looked so delicious that I was running to the kitchen to create my version before he had finished his demonstration. As a result, mine was entirely different from his, but equally scrumptious.

It is not as complicated as it looks, and although it may necessitate a visit to the Thai shop, it's well worth the effort. It's the chopping and preparing of the ingredients that takes a little time; the stir-frying itself is very quick.

For 2 starter size helpings, use:

100–125 g (4 oz) bean thread noodles or rice vermicelli
1 x 15 ml spoon (1 tablespoon)vegetable or sesame seed oil
4 medium/large spring onions including green part (or shallots), finely sliced
1 large clove garlic, crushed
1 small red chilli, dried or fresh, finely chopped or crumbled
1 x 15 ml spoon (1 tablespoon) fresh ginger root, finely chopped or grated
3 kaffir lime leaves, finely slivered using kitchen scissors
175 g (6 oz) tinned crab, drained of its brine
1 egg, beaten
2 x 15 ml spoons (2 tablespoons) light soy sauce
3 x 15 ml spoons (3 tablespoons) fresh coriander leaves, chopped
50 g (2 oz) roasted, crushed fresh peanuts, *or* 2 x 15 ml spoons (2 tablespoons) toasted sesame seeds

Soak the noodles in a bowl of tepid water for about 15–20 minutes. Drain. At the last minute, before adding to the other ingredients, drop the noodles into a pan or bowl of boiling water. Leave for about 30 seconds, drain, and then add to other ingredients.

Stir-fry the spring onion, garlic, chilli, ginger and kaffir lime leaves in the oil, until the spring onion starts to soften and darken in colour. Add the crab, stir-fry for another 10 seconds and then add the cooked noodles and stir-fry again. Throw on the egg and stir-fry briskly as it cooks. Add the light soy sauce and most of the coriander. Turn over a few more times and then serve immediately, with the crushed nuts (or sesame seeds) and remaining coriander sprinkled on top.

95 Thai rice noodles with salmon or bean curd, bean sprouts, mushrooms, red pepper, coriander and toasted sesame seeds

Don't be put off by the length of this recipe. It may even seem a little complicated the first time you make it, but you will soon pick up the ideas and methods.

The cooking itself is very quick, so the trick is to have all the ingredients ready, sliced and prepared and waiting, so that you do not have to turn off the heat whilst you run to the fridge for forgotten ingredients.

This is an excellent general Thai rice noodle stir-fry recipe. Use it as a basis on which to experiment, trying out other vegetables (always finely sliced), other fish or tofu products and even other kinds of nuts and herbs. For example, you can substitute shitake, oyster, and *marron* mushrooms mixed together for the mushrooms.

For the best results – use a wok!

For 2–3 main course helpings, use:

225 g (8 oz) dried wide, flat rice noodles
50 g (2 oz) unsalted fresh peanuts, shelled
25 g (1 oz) sesame seeds
2 small fillets of salmon (75 g/3 oz each), *or* use
  175 ml/6 oz firm tofu
3 x 15 ml spoons (3 tablespoons) sesame seed or
  vegetable oil
50 g (2 oz) shallots or spring onions, finely sliced
2 cloves garlic, crushed
1 or 2 dried chillies (to taste), chopped or crumbled
1 x 15 ml spoon (1 tablespoon) fresh root ginger, finely
  chopped or grated
4 kaffir lime leaves, finely slivered with scissors
10 cm (4 inches) lemon grass stalk, bruised with a rolling

pin, then finely sliced

100–125 g (4 oz) red pepper, finely sliced

100–125 g (4 oz) mushrooms, finely sliced

100–125 g (4 oz) bean sprouts, *or* substitute Savoy cabbage, or Chinese cabbage, finely sliced

3 x 15 ml spoons (3 tablespoons) light soy sauce *or* 2 x 15 ml spoons (2 tablespoons) dark soy sauce

3 x 15 ml spoons (3 tablespoons) vegetable stock or water

1 x 10 ml spoon (1 dessertspoon) vinegar

1 x 5 ml spoon (1 teaspoon) caster sugar

1 x 15 ml spoon (1 tablespoon) light fish sauce (optional)

3 x 15 ml spoons (3 tablespoons) fresh coriander, chopped

Soak the rice noodles in lukewarm water for 20 minutes.

Roast the peanuts on a baking tray, in a hot oven for about 10 or 15 minutes or until they begin to darken in colour. Remove from the oven, allow to cool and then remove the husks. Crush in a pestle and mortar or put in a plastic bag and crush with a rolling pin, or meat tenderiser.

Dry-fry the sesame seeds in a small, non-stick pan, watching carefully to make sure that they don't burn!

Remove any skin from the salmon (if using). Cut the salmon or tofu into small chunks about 3 cm/1¼ inches square. Sauté in a non-stick pan, if possible, in 1 x 15 ml spoon (1 tablespoon) of the sesame seed oil with half the toasted sesame seeds and a little of the chopped shallots until nicely browned on the outside. (If you are using salmon, be careful not to overcook as it will then become too dry.)

Stir-fry the remaining shallots or spring onions with the garlic and the chilli for 10 or 15 seconds in the remaining oil, over a fairly high heat. Throw in the ginger, kaffir lime leaves and lemon grass and stir-fry for another 20 or so seconds. Add the red pepper and stir-fry until the pepper softens. Now add the mushrooms, continue to stir-fry until they darken in colour and then add the bean sprouts. Stir-fry for another 20 or 30 seconds.

Drain the soaked rice noodles, put back in the bowl and

pour boiling water over them. Leave them for 30 seconds and then drain again.

Add the partially cooked rice noodles to the contents of the wok, toss together quickly and then add the light (or dark) soy sauce, the vegetable stock, vinegar, caster sugar, light fish sauce, if using, and stir-fry together for another 20 or 30 seconds.

Divide the noodle mixture into individual bowls, scatter the salmon or tofu chunks on top, sprinkle over the toasted peanuts, coriander and remaining sesame seeds. Serve with chopsticks or forks (the Thais don't use chopsticks).

Kids

- Take trouble to make sure that you are cooking with enough water. If water goes cloudy, boil up a kettle and add more boiling water.
- If you think the pasta and sauce might turn out a little dry, some people suggest draining the pasta quickly and leaving in some of the cooking water.
- Instead of serving freshly grated Parmesan, try putting a lump of Parmesan and a grater on the table so people can grate their own.
- *Always* taste the pasta before adding grated cheese. It often doesn't need it, especially any pasta with fish, and that includes anchovies.
- Always feel free to *substitute*. That's what all the best Italian cooks do – they make the sauce with whatever is in the house, the garden or available that week in the market.
- Almost all my ingredients are optional, apart from the pasta itself! Experiment with what you have and what you like, and invent your own sauces, using my recipes as a base.
- The secret of a good tomato sauce is never burning the garlic. It should always retain its white colour. If the garlic goes crispy and brown, take it out and start again!
- Adjust the chilli according to taste. It is very hard to give an accurate measurement as chillies vary. The saying is, the smaller the hotter.
- Always remember to use lots and lots of fast-boiling, lightly salted water to cook your pasta.
- If your pasta is soggy and tasteless, or continues cooking after you have drained it, here are some possible reasons:

    You've overcooked it;

    You've used an unreliable brand. Use good-quality Italian pasta, for example, de Cecco or Barilla (not Buitoni) or experiment with your local supermarket produce until you find one that works well for you.
- If your pasta is soft on the outside but still hard in the centre it could be that you are not using enough water to cook it in.
- Find a brand of pasta that you like and stock up on it. I recommend F. lli de Cecco, Barilla (not Buitoni) and Marks and Spencer dried fresh egg pasta.
- If you use a good brand of pasta and cook it correctly (with lots of salted, boiling water until it is 'al dente') it will not go mushy on you – you can even drain it, toss it with a spoonful of oil and heat it up later or the following day.
- Feel free to experiment. Be brave. Open the fridge and make a sauce with whatever falls out.
- Stock up on store cupboard standbys from the Introduction and you will always be able to dish up a meal for friends at short notice.
- If you are partial to one of the spicy tomato sauces make extra and freeze in cupfuls. Add a little extra oil after defrosting.
- Buy herbs in pots at your local supermarket and keep them on your kitchen windowsill.
- Buy pesto sauce from the chilled section of the supermarket and freeze in ice cube trays. Decant into a plastic bag and keep frozen for future use.
- I heard Delia Smith the other day on television saying, 'Life is too short to roast a red pepper.' All I can say is I disagree – totally – and I am quite a lazy cook and believe in dishes that can be prepared quickly with the minimum amount of fuss. I *don't* find roasting red peppers a hardship. It's easy-peasy and quick. Just follow my instructions.

Introduction

It seems to be a modern phenomenon that kids love pasta. And more and more are turning to vegetarianism of their own volition, at a surprisingly young age.

Very young children seem to prefer just a little grated cheese or tomato purée on their pasta. My stepsons used to live on the simpler tomato sauce (and Bolognese, because they are *not* vegetarian, from my first book, *Pastability*). Their usually small appetites were miraculously transformed at the sight of pasta and they would eat an enormous helping with a wary eye on the pot (and each other) for who was going to get first go at seconds. It was not until they were over ten or eleven that they started to appreciate the flavours of garlic, chilli, herbs and the more varied sauces. By the age of about fifteen or sixteen I reckon teenagers move on to more or less adult recipes and start to appreciate one's culinary skills and all the hard work that goes into feeding a family.

Choosing recipes for your children depends on adapting these ideas to incorporate the ingredients they like and avoiding those they can't stand. I do *not* believe in forcing children to eat things they don't like. Life is too short and, on the whole, I think children have a fairly healthy instinct for what's good for them, only distorted by *sugar*, which is more a drug than a food. I couldn't stand dried apricots and cinnamon and remember to this day the pain of being forced to eat apricots at my school. I resorted to salting them until I could no longer taste the apricot.

Wherever possible, make a large quantity of what your child likes and freeze it in small portions.

For teenagers and older kids, just look through the book and find what you think will suit them. In my experience, most of them are fussy and faddy and so I reckon that it would be a waste of time for me to recommend particular recipes!

96 Bows with butter, carrots and orange

An easy children's recipe. For a variation, add a couple of chopped tomatoes, or steamed broccoli florets, or maybe some chives or parsley or basil, and/or a tablespoon (1 x 15 ml spoon) of cream cheese.

For 3–4 child size helpings, use:

325 g (12 oz) carrots, scraped and then finely sliced,
   or chopped
1 x 15 ml (1 tablespoon) butter
50 g (2 oz) onion, finely chopped (optional)
1 x 15 ml spoon (1 tablespoon) orange juice
some grated zest of orange (optional)
225 g (8 oz) bows or wholewheat shells
1 or 2 x 15 ml spoons (1 or 2 tablespoons) grated
   Parmesan or Cheddar

Boil the chopped carrots in a little salted water until cooked but not mushy – remove whilst they still retain their bright orange colour. Drain and put aside.

Sauté the onion (if using) in the butter until softened and translucent. Throw in the parboiled carrot and sauté for another half minute. Add the orange juice (and zest, or tomato, or herbs if using).

Meanwhile, cook the pasta in salted, boiling water until 'al dente'. Drain and put back into the pan with the sauce.

Toss the pasta and sauce together and serve immediately, with or without grated cheese sprinkled on top.

97 Macaroni cheese

With the choice of exotic and interesting recipes in this book I hope you won't be making this dish for the grown-ups, but just for the children still at the age where they like simple food and flavours.

It is very hard to predict how many small people this serving will feed as children's appetites vary so considerably. My stepchildren used to eat very small portions of everything, except pasta, which they devoured by the heaped plateful.

You could try making this dish incorporating your child's favourite vegetable, for example, 50 g (2 oz) cooked peas, broccoli, spinach or carrots.

For children who are allergic to dairy produce, you could make this dish substituting margarine, vegetable or olive oil for the butter; goat's milk or soya milk for the milk; and goat's or sheep's cheese for the Cheddar.

For *approximately* 4 main course helpings, use:

> 225 g (8 oz) macaroni, small shells or quills (plain or wholewheat)

For the béchamel sauce
> 25 g (1 oz) butter
> 25 g (1 oz) flour
> 575 ml (1 pint) milk (full-cream or semi-skimmed)
> 1 pinch mustard powder
> salt and pepper (optional)
> 100–125 g (4 oz) Cheddar cheese, grated (or substitute Cheshire or Emmenthal)

Cook the béchamel sauce as directed on page 224, using the simpler method (2). Stir in half the cheese and the pinch of mustard powder, and season to taste.

Meanwhile, cook the pasta in plenty of boiling water until 'al dente' (if anything, a fraction undercooked – if it is borderline overcooked at this stage then it will be horrendously mushy and white at the final stage). Drain and put back in the pan with a little oil or butter.

Pour over the sauce and mix together. Put into an ovenproof dish. Sprinkle over the remaining cheese, and bake in a preheated moderate oven (190°C/375°F/gas mark 5) for about half an hour.

If the top is not yet sufficiently browned, then brown it further under the grill.

98 Cheese and tomato macaroni cheese

This is really just macaroni cheese livened up with a couple of layers of tomato sauce.

If this looks like too much trouble, then go back to the basic recipe (recipe 97, on page 209), and take the easy way out: mix a little tomato purée (about 2 x 15 ml spoons/2 tablespoons) with some (a quarter or less) of the béchamel and add a tomato layer thus.

For children who are allergic to dairy produce, you could make this dish substituting margarine, vegetable or olive oil for the butter; goat's milk or soya milk for the milk; and goat's or sheep's cheese for the Cheddar.

For *approximately* 4 main course helpings, use:

225 g (8 oz) macaroni, small shells or quills
(plain or wholewheat)

For the béchamel sauce
25 g (1 oz) butter
25 g (1 oz) flour
575 ml (1 pint) milk (full-cream or semi-skimmed)
1 pinch mustard powder
salt and pepper (optional)

For the tomato sauce
1 x 15 ml spoon (1 tablespoon) olive or vegetable oil
½ clove garlic, crushed (optional)
¼ dried chilli, crumbled (very optional!)
200 g (7 oz) tinned tomatoes, coarsely chopped
½ x 15 ml spoon (½ tablespoon) tomato purée (optional)
1 x 5 ml spoon (1 teaspoon) dried oregano or fresh herbs
from the garden
½ x 5 ml spoon (½ teaspoon) sugar
100-125 g (4 oz) Cheddar cheese, grated
(or substitute Cheshire or Emmenthal)

Cook the béchamel sauce as directed on page 224, using the simpler method (2). Stir in half the cheese and the pinch of mustard powder, and season to taste.

Sauté the garlic and chilli (if using) for a minute or so, taking care not to burn it. Add the tomatoes, tomato purée, sugar and herbs and simmer for 10 to 15 minutes.

Meanwhile, cook the pasta in plenty of boiling water until 'al dente' (if anything, a fraction undercooked – if it is borderline overcooked at this stage then it will be horrendously mushy and white at the final stage). Drain and put back in the pan with a little oil or butter.

Pour over the sauce and mix together. Put a layer of the pasta and béchamel into the bottom of an ovenproof dish. Spread over a thin layer of tomato sauce, another layer of pasta with béchamel, then tomato and so on until you run out of ingredients. Sprinkle over the remaining cheese, and bake in a preheated moderate oven (190°C/375°F/gas mark 5) for about half an hour.

If the top is not yet sufficiently browned, then brown it further under the grill.

99 Bows with very easy tomato and mascarpone (or cream cheese) sauce

Very quick and easy indeed, very tasty and surprisingly rich. If you find it is too rich, then add more water and apple juice, or a couple of ounces of chopped, fresh or tinned tomatoes.

For 2–4 main course (child size) servings:

1 x 15 ml spoon (1 tablespoon) olive or vegetable oil
½ clove garlic, crushed (optional – to taste)
tiny pinch chilli powder or dried chilli (very optional)
2 x 15 ml spoons (2 tablespoons) tomato purée
2 x 15 ml spoons (2 tablespoons) mascarpone or cream cheese
4 x 15 ml spoons (4 tablespoons) water and apple juice mixed (or use just water)
175 g (6 oz) bows
freshly grated cheese (optional)

Sauté the garlic and chilli, if using, in the oil in a small pan over a low flame. Stir in the tomato purée, and then the mascarpone or cream cheese, and then finally the apple juice/water. Heat through.

Meanwhile, cook the pasta in plenty of salted, boiling water until 'al dente'. Drain, and then put back in the pan. Pour over the sauce, mix together and serve immediately with extra grated cheese on the side if you like.

100 Angel hair with butter, egg and Parmesan cheese

This is a quick one for the kiddies, given to me by Idelma who brought me up when I was a small child. She feeds this to her grandchildren, who simply adore it. For a grown-up version you could consider adding a pinch of flaked chilli, or some 'nori' seaweed (see recipe 87, page 182), finely slivered with kitchen scissors.

For 2–4 main course (child size) helpings:

    1 large egg (preferably free range)
    35 g (1½ oz) Parmesan, finely grated
        (or substitute a very mild Cheddar, or Emmenthal)
    salt and pepper
    100–125 g (4 oz) angel hair
        (or vermicelli, cappelini, spaghettini or small macaroni)
    1 x 15 ml spoon (1 tablespoon) butter

Break the egg into a small bowl and beat with a fork, adding half the cheese and beating again. Season to taste.

Meanwhile, cook the pasta in plenty of salted, boiling water until 'al dente'. Drain and put back into the pan over a low heat. Toss with the 1 x 15 ml spoon (1 tablespoon) butter, and then add the beaten egg and cheese and quickly toss again before the egg has cooked. Serve immediately with the remaining cheese sprinkled on top.

101 Quills with tuna, spring onions and mayonnaise

Another recipe given to me by our assistant, Louise Arthur. I added the celery, which is why I have made it optional.

For a more grown-up version, add ¼ x 5 ml spoon (¼ teaspoon) curry powder and 1 x 5 ml spoon (1 teaspoon) apricot jam stirred into the mayonnaise.

For 4 starter size helpings, use:

200 g (7 oz) tin tuna, drained
75–100 g (3 oz) spring onions, sliced into rings
2 x 15 ml spoons (2 tablespoons) mayonnaise
75–100 g (3 oz) celery, finely sliced (optional)
325 g (12 oz) quills
15 g (½ oz) butter

Flake the tuna in a bowl. Add the mayonnaise and mix well. Add the spring onions and celery, if using, and set aside.

Meanwhile, cook the pasta in plenty of salted, boiling water until it is 'al dente'. Drain and add the butter to the pasta, allowing it to melt. Add the tuna mix to the pasta, stir and serve.

102 Bows with tomato sauce and vegetarian sausages

Something simple and tasty to feed to the kids. I recommend using Cauldron Foods' premium vegetarian sausages. They're very tasty, a nice texture, and 'brown' well. If you find yourself using sausages which are not so spicy, then you may want to consider adding a small pinch of chilli powder and ½ clove of crushed garlic at the sautéed onion stage, depending on *your* children's tastes.

About 4 child size portions:

2 vegetarian sausages
1 x 15 ml spoon (1 tablespoon) olive oil or butter
75–100 g (3 oz) onion, finely sliced or chopped
1 medium tin (400 g/14 oz) chopped Italian tomatoes
½ x 5 ml spoon (½ teaspoon) sugar
½ x 5 ml spoon (½ teaspoon) dried herbs *or* 1 x 15 ml spoon (1 tablespoon) chopped herbs (optional)
225–325 g (8–12 oz) bows
grated Cheddar cheese (optional)

Grill or fry the vegetarian sausages according to the instructions on the packet. Cut into small slices or chunks.

Sauté the onion in the oil or butter until it turns translucent or golden. Add the tomatoes, sugar and herbs and simmer for another 10 minutes, stirring frequently.

Meanwhile, cook the pasta in plenty of boiling, salted water until it is 'al dente'. Drain and toss with the tomato sauce and chopped vegetarian sausage.

Serve with grated Cheddar cheese on the side or sprinkled over the top of each serving (optional).

103 Twists with sweetcorn, tuna and cheese

Very quick and easy. You could make this dish substituting a couple of vegetarian sausages, grilled, and then chopped or sliced, for the tuna fish. For a variation try this recipe using coloured pasta, or an unusual shape such as the 'cartwheels' (made by B. de Cecco), a big favourite of my stepchildren, Oscar and Rupert.

For 4 children's size portions:

    225–325 g (8–12 oz) twists
    1 x 15 ml spoon (1 tablespoon) olive oil or butter
    200 g (7 oz) tin tuna (in brine or oil), drained
    200 g (7 oz) tinned sweetcorn kernels
    75–100 g (3 oz) grated Cheddar cheese (mild), *or* substitute
        another cheese, such as Emmenthal or Cheshire

Cook the pasta in plenty of boiling, salted water until 'al dente'. Drain and toss with the oil (or butter), tuna, sweetcorn and cheese over a low heat until well mixed, or else serve the grated cheese on the side in a little bowl.

Serve immediately.

Etceteras

104 My salad

Without wishing to be immodest, everybody compliments me on my salad dressing. I should really *sell* the recipe or the dressing, bottled, but here I am giving it away in my book.

Fine-tune the quantities to *your* taste.

For the vinaigrette
   2 x 15 ml spoons (2 tablespoons) balsamic (or red wine) vinegar

   6 x 15 ml spoons (6 tablespoons) very good olive oil (such as Waitrose Extra Virgin olive oil)

   1 x 5 ml spoon (1 teaspoon) mustard (English, Dijon or grainy mustard)

   ¼ x 5 ml spoon (¼ teaspoon) curry powder (optional)

   small pinch grated nutmeg (optional)

   1 x 5 ml spoon (1 teaspoon) caster sugar

   1 or 2 cloves garlic, crushed (optional)

   sea salt and freshly ground black pepper

For the salad
Most big supermarkets now sell wonderful bags of mixed lettuces. These tend to be pricey, but very easy! Or be inventive and make your own with whatever takes your fancy and/or is available in your local shops. Choose crisp lettuces, such as iceberg and cos; lettuces to add colour and different textures, such as radicchio (an Italian red lettuce) and lollo biondo (a rather frizzy green and yellow lettuce); lamb's lettuce; sliced endive; watercress; baby spinach leaves; chopped celery; and spring onion. Best of all, if you can lay your hands on it, is rocket (arugula). And what about adding some of your favourite fresh herb? I would recommend tarragon, coriander, thyme (in very small quantities).

Put the vinaigrette ingredients in a mug or bowl and beat together with a fork. Pour over the salad *just before* serving and mix together with salad spoon and fork or (clean) hands.

105 Home-made tagliatelle

I have always strongly resisted the idea of making my own pasta. My view has always been that whilst there are such good products available on the open market, such as the Barilla and F. lli de Cecco dried tagliatelles, and since the supermarkets have so improved their product, what would be the point? But finally I decided that I really should try cooking fresh pasta for myself so that I could honestly test the product and decide whether or not to recommend the whole procedure to others.

I set out to buy a pasta machine. I asked around, and let it be known that I required the machine that did the most amount of work for me. What was the point, I argued, in getting a machine that simply rolled out the pasta, if that meant that I still had to knead the wretched stuff for ten minutes? Mr Pyemont of Melrose, Scotland, from whom I buy my excellent coffee and who turned out to be an expert on the subject of fresh pasta, recommended the Pastamatic Extruder and I subsequently bought the machine direct from a distributor. I have since discovered that the machine is also available in some major stores such as Harrods.

My next mission was to find the right flour. No soft-wheat bread flour for me; I required the genuine Italian article. My friend Mrs Roche, manager of Waitrose in the Finchley Road, led me to her Italian produce shelves where, to my amazement, I found 'Farina "00" di grano tenero' made by Ferrari of Parma. (Well, they make good *cars* anyway.) I duly purchased a bag of the stuff and now there were no excuses left.

The machine I purchased works like a Magimix combined with a mincing machine. The worst problem was understanding the instructions for putting the damn thing together. Like most people I know, I have a resistance to following instruction booklets and normally there is a point at which they seem to break into Chinese or jargonese. However, once I knuckled down to it, it wasn't so hard, just tedious. From then on the going was comparatively easy.

My friend David Meredith, who adores fresh pasta, helped me. Following the recipe in the instruction book, we measured out the flour, measured out the eggs in a special plastic measuring jug (much more exact than just specifying a number of eggs), fed the stuff into the machine and more or less sat back and waited. After five minutes the mixture arrived at the correct texture and then we switched it to 'producing pasta' mode. This was the exciting part. Tagliatelle emerged from the 'mincing' section – about eight strands of the stuff as we stood eagerly watching, knife poised to cut off the strands when they reached the required length. We then hung the tagliatelle over the kitchen broom suspended between two kitchen chairs and covered with dishcloths. This was not strictly required by the recipe but had been recommended by Mr Pyemont. The most difficult bit was persuading David to wait half an hour or so before we threw the pasta into the boiling water.

We ate it simply, with just butter, pepper and Parmesan. And I must admit, it was totally delicious. Whether this was just because we had had to work so hard and wait so long for our plate of pasta, or whether it was because the finished product is superior, I really couldn't tell you.

Mail order coffee suppliers
Pyemont & Company
Hassendean Station Denholm
Hawick TD9 8PX
Tel. 01450 870670

106 Recipe for béchamel sauce

Béchamel sauce is used in a number of the recipes. To make the sauce, use the quantities specified for the recipe you are following, and proceed as follows:

Version 1

Put the milk into a pan with 2 bay leaves, half an onion and a few peppercorns. Bring to just below the boil, then remove from the heat and leave to infuse for 15 minutes. Strain.

Melt the butter slowly in a heavy-bottomed pan, taking care not to let it burn. Mix in the flour, stirring well with a wooden spoon. Add the milk, a little at a time, stirring constantly until the lumps disappear and the sauce thickens. If the sauce ingredients include mustard powder and/or grated cheese, stir them in when you have used up all the milk.

Version 2 (a quicker method)

If you are in a hurry, proceed as above, but omit the bay leaves, onion and peppercorns and use milk straight from the bottle or carton.

Note: If the sauce develops lumps, beat it with an egg whisk or electric hand beater. I usually whisk it anyway, for good measure!

Index

Main ingredients are indicated by **bold** type

cheese *see* blue, Boursin, Brie,
Cambiola, Cambozola,
Camembert, Cheddar,
Cheshire, cottage, cream,
curd, Dolcelatte, Emmenthal,
feta, fromage frais, goat's,
Gorgonzola, mascarpone,
Mozzarella, 'quark', ricotta,
Stilton

Cheshire cheese:
Aubergine, tomato and cheese
mould ('sformata') with pesto
sauce and toasted pine
kernels, 90–92
Cheese and tomato macaroni
cheese, 211–12
Macaroni cheese, 209–10
Rigatoni with onions, cheese
and olives, 116
Twists with sweetcorn, tuna and
cheese, 217

chickpeas, 123
Cold pasta salad with chickpeas, boiled eggs, cherry
tomatoes, walnuts, herbs and
capers, 103–4
Shells with spicy Indian
aubergine, tomato, red
pepper and chickpeas,
117–18

chillies:
Spaghetti Machiavelli with king
prawns, mushrooms, chilli,
garlic and basil, 151–2
Spaghetti with oil, garlic and
chilli, 29
Spaghetti with puréed roast red
pepper, chilli and tomato,
111–12

chives, 55, 76, 78
Twists with smoked salmon, red
peppers, chives, pine kernels,
cream and vodka, 165–6

clams:
Frank's spaghetti vongole, 149

cockles:

Linguini with tomato and
seafood, 153–4

coconut, 181, 194
Green Thai aubergine coconut
curry, 171–2
Spicy Thai spring greens with
kaffir lime leaves and coconut
milk, 175–6
Vegetarian red coconut curry,
served with noodles, 173–4

cod, 194

conchiglie, 2

coriander:
Bean thread or rice vermicelli
stir-fried with crab, coriander
and kaffir lime leaves, 200–1
Japanese buckwheat noodles
with shitake and oyster
mushrooms, ginger, cour-
gettes, black and white
sesame seeds, tofu and nori
(toasted seaweed) or coriander, 184–6
Tagliatelle (or frills) in a carrot,
parsnip and cumin soup with
courgettes, asparagus (or
cabbage or broccoli) and
coriander, 110–11
Thai fried rice noodles ('Pad
Thai') with bean sprouts,
peanuts and coriander, 177–9
Thai green curry with salmon
(or white fish), courgettes,
aubergines, ginger, noodles
and coriander, 193–5
Thai rice noodles with salmon
or bean curd, bean sprouts,
mushrooms, red pepper,
coriander and toasted sesame
seeds, 202–4
Thai spring rolls filled with
bean thread (or rice vermicelli), vegetables, coriander
and kaffir lime leaves,
180–81

cottage cheese, 68, 93, 100

228

cheese, 74–5

Tagliatelle (or quills) with roast mixed vegetables, 80–81

Thai rice noodles with salmon or bean curd, bean sprouts, mushrooms, red pepper, coriander and toasted sesame seeds, 202–4

Thai spring rolls filled with bean thread (or rice vermicelli), vegetables, coriander and kaffir lime leaves, 180–81

Twists with red and yellow roast peppers, caramelised onions and goat's cheese (or feta), 70–71

Twists with smoked salmon, red peppers, chives, pine kernels, cream and vodka, 165–6

Vegetarian red coconut curry, served with noodles, 173–4

peppers, yellow, 115

Twists with red and yellow roast peppers, caramelised onions and goat's cheese (or feta), 70–71

pesto sauce, 41, 121

Aubergine, tomato and cheese mould ('sformata') with pesto sauce and toasted pine kernels, 90–92

Bows with very quick and easy tomato, sun-dried tomato and pesto sauce, 57

Courgette, mushroom, red pepper and sweet potato lasagne with pesto sauce and pine kernels, 85–7

Rigatoni with tomato and pesto sauce and optional pine kernels, basil and/or ricotta, 53–4

Tagliatelle with creamy pesto and basil, 84

Twists with pesto, mascarpone

cheese (or crème fraîche) and ricotta, 105

pine kernels, 70, 78, 100

Aubergine, tomato and cheese mould ('sformata') with pesto sauce and toasted pine kernels, 90–92

Courgette, mushroom, red pepper and sweet potato lasagne with pesto sauce and pine kernels, 85–7

Linguini with tomatoes, anchovies, olives, capers and optional sun-dried tomatoes and pine kernels, 142–3

Quills with creamy tomato sauce, Camembert, Emmenthal and toasted pine kernels, 51–2

Rigatoni with tomato and pesto sauce and optional pine kernels, basil and/or ricotta, 53–4

Saskia's twists with anchovies, sun-dried tomatoes, red pepper, chopped herbs and roasted pine kernels, 26–7

Twists with smoked salmon, red peppers, chives, pine kernels, cream and vodka, 165–6

pine nuts:

Twists with pumpkin (or butternut squash), herbs and pine nuts, 76–7

pistachio nuts:

Quills with celery, Stilton, mascarpone (or cream), vodka, fresh herbs and optional pistachios, 102

porcini mushrooms:

Aubergine, porcini, leek or pea mould ('sformata'), 110

Home-made tagliatelle with dried porcini (or cep) mushrooms, crème fraîche (or cream) and walnuts, 119

Tagliatelle with leeks and
porcini mushrooms, 115
prawns:
Ba mee nah talay (Thai fresh
egg noodles with seafood),
197–9
Quills or shells with avocado,
lemon and optional shrimps
or prawns, 131–32
Spaghetti Machiavelli with king
prawns, mushrooms, chilli,
garlic and basil, 151–2
Thai red curry with white fish,
prawns, crushed peanuts and
noodles, 196
pumpkin:
Linguini (or spaghetti) with
courgettes, aubergine, roasted
red peppers, and pumpkin (or
butternut squash), 78–9
Twists with pumpkin (or butternut squash), herbs and pine
nuts, 76–7

'quark', 68
quills, 29, 111, 153, 155, 192,
209, 211
Aubergine, tomato and cheese
mould ('sformata') with pesto
sauce and toasted pine
kernels, 90–92
Basic Italian tomato sauce,
125–6
Penne primavera, 63–4
Tagliatelle (or quills) with roast
mixed vegetables, 80–81
Quills with butter, anchovies,
garlic, red pepper, walnuts
and crème fraîche, 47–8
Quills with celery, Stilton, mascarpone (or cream), vodka, fresh
herbs and optional pistachios,
102
Quills with green beans, courgette,
mushrooms, tomatoes, butter
beans, pesto sauce and

fromage frais, 41–2
Quills with courgettes (or green
beans), blue cheese, herbs
and cream, 49–50
Quills with crab and creamy
tomato sauce, 160–61
Quills with creamy tomato sauce,
Camembert, Emmenthal and
toasted pine kernels, 51–2
Quills or shells with avocado,
lemon and optional shrimps
or prawns, 131–2
Quills with smoked salmon,
vodka and cream, 130
Quills with spicy Indian tomato
sauce, tofu and sesame seeds,
82–3
Quills with spicy tomatoes and
aubergine, 113–14
Quills with Stilton, sage and
cream, 24
Quills with tuna, spring onions
and mayonnaise, 215
Quills with vodka, tomato and
cream, 25

ravioli:
Shop-bought fresh stuffed ravioli with roast vegetables,
Mozzarella and herbs,
120–22
ricotta cheese:
Rigatoni with tomato and pesto
sauce and optional pine
kernels, basil and/or ricotta,
53–4
Twists with pesto, mascarpone
cheese (or crème fraîche) and
ricotta, 105
rigatoni, 2
Rigatoni with creamy crab,
tomato, avocado and sage,
155–6
Rigatoni with onions, cheese and
olives, 116
Rigatoni with red pepper, toma-

Shells with scallops, cream and
curry, 158
Shells with spicy Indian aubergine,
tomato, red pepper and
chickpeas, 117–18
shrimps:
Quills or shells with avocado,
lemon and optional shrimps
or prawns, 131–2
Thai red curry with white fish,
prawns, crushed peanuts and
noodles, 196
soured cream, 67
soy bean sauce, 198
spaghetti, 135, 139, 142, 153
Frank's spaghetti vongole, 149
freezing, 8
Gian Carlo Menotti's 'spaghetti
dei poveri' with tomatoes,
parsley and garlic, 36–7
Linguini (or spaghetti) with
courgettes, aubergine, roasted
red peppers, and pumpkin (or
butternut squash), 78–9
Spaghetti with anchovies and
mushrooms, 140–41
Spaghetti with anchovies, olives,
tomatoes and capers, 147–8
Spaghetti Machiavelli with king
prawns, mushrooms, chilli,
garlic and basil, 151–2
Spaghetti with oil, garlic and
chilli, 29
Spaghetti with oil, garlic and
herbs, 28
Spaghetti with puréed roast red
pepper, chilli and tomato,
111–12
Spaghetti with salmon, cream and
tarragon, 159
Spaghetti with simple traditional
tomato sauce, 106–7
Spaghetti with smoked salmon
and cream, 129
Spaghetti with tarragon and
lemon, 34

Spaghetti with tomatoes, red
pepper, olives and Mozzarella
cheese, 74–5
spaghettini, 2, 34, 129, 147, 149,
214
Buckwheat noodles (or spaghettini) with ginger, soy sauce,
orange, tofu and toasted
sesame seeds, 187
Spaghettini with lightly fried courgettes and herbs, 21–2
Spaghettini with red caviar, 139
spinach, 167
The Actors' Centre lentil and
spinach lasagne, 68–9
Baked tagliatelle with spinach,
eggs and cheese, 95–6
Bows with spinach, mascarpone
(or cream cheese) and roast
red peppers, 100–1
Salmon, spinach, leek, mushroom and tarragon lasagne,
162–4
Spinach lasagne, 65–6
Spinach cannelloni, 93–4
spring greens:
Gnocchetti with spring greens,
red pepper and Mozzarella,
38
Spicy Thai spring greens with
kaffir lime leaves and coconut
milk, 175–6
spring onions:
Quills with tuna, spring onions
and mayonnaise, 215
spring roll pastry, 181
squid:
Ba mee nah talay (Thai fresh
egg noodles with seafood),
197–9
Linguini with tomato and
seafood, 153–4
Stilton cheese, 49
Quills with celery, Stilton,
mascarpone (or cream),
vodka, fresh herbs and